DENALI

Volume 15, Number 3 / 1988
ALASKA GEOGRAPHIC®

The Alaska Geographic Society

To teach many more to better know and use our natural resources

Editor: Penny Rennick
Associate Editor: Kathy Doogan
Editorial Assistant: Laurie Thompson
Designer: Sandra Harner

THE ALASKA GEOGRAPHIC SOCIETY is a non-profit organization exploring new frontiers of knowledge across the lands of the Polar Rim, learning how other men and other countries live in their Norths, putting the geography book back in the classroom, exploring new methods of teaching and learning — sharing in the excitement of discovery in man's wonderful new world north of 51°16.

MEMBERS OF THE SOCIETY receive ALASKA GEOGRAPHIC, a quality magazine that devotes each quarterly issue to monographic in-depth coverage of a northern geographic region or resource-oriented subject.

MEMBERSHIP DUES in The Alaska Geographic Society are $30 per year; $34 to non-U.S. addresses. (Eighty percent of each year's dues is for a one-year subscription to ALASKA GEOGRAPHIC.) Order from The Alaska Geographic Society, Box 93370, Anchorage, AK 99509-3370; phone (907) 258-2515.

PRICE TO NONMEMBERS THIS ISSUE, $14.95 ($18.95 Canadian)

MATERIALS SOUGHT: The editors of ALASKA GEOGRAPHIC seek a wide variety of informative material on the lands north of 51°16 on geographic subjects — anything to do with resources and their uses (with heavy emphasis on quality color photography) — from all the lands of the Polar Rim and the economically related North Pacific Rim. We cannot be responsible for submissions not accompanied by sufficient postage for return by certified mail. Payments are made for all material upon publication.

CHANGE OF ADDRESS: The post office does not automatically forward ALASKA GEOGRAPHIC when you move. To ensure continuous service, notify us six weeks before moving. Send us your new address and zip code (and moving date), your old address and zip code, and if possible send a mailing label from a copy of ALASKA GEOGRAPHIC. Send this information to ALASKA GEOGRAPHIC Mailing Offices, 130 Second Avenue South, Edmonds, WA 98020-9989.

MAILING LISTS: We have begun making our members' names and addresses available to carefully screened publications and companies whose products and activities may be of interest to you. If you would prefer not to receive such mailings, please so advise us, and include your mailing label (or your name and address if label is not available).

ABOUT THIS ISSUE: Many contributed to this review of Alaska's heartland, the high country wilderness of Denali. The geographical and historical overview comes from Elaine Rhode, and former Denali ranger Kim Heacox calls upon his experience with scientific writing to describe how a mountain's elevation is determined. Karen Jettmar gives a firsthand account of her ascent of Mount McKinley, and long-time Fairbanks resident and geologist Thomas K. Bundtzen thoroughly reviews the historical and contemporary status of mining in the Kantishna district. Another Fairbanks resident, Celia Hunter, describes the founding and early years at the wilderness retreat of Camp Denali.

No discussion of Denali country would be complete without mentioning Hudson Stuck and Bradford Washburn. Stuck's party made the first ascent of Mount McKinley and his account of reaching the ultimate height is included here. Decades later, Bradford Washburn made numerous ascents of the mountain, photographing and charting its flanks with a scientist's eye. Washburn's achievements, as well as those of others who have come face to face with Denali, The High One, are chronicled in "Highlights in the History of Mount McKinley," excerpted from *A Tourist Guide to Mount McKinley* by Bradford Washburn.

As always, we thank the many fine photographers whose images have captured the spirit of Denali country. We are grateful to Thomas K. Buntzen and the staff at Denali National Park and Denali State Park for their help with research and their review of portions of the manuscript.

The Library of Congress has cataloged this serial publication as follows:

Alaska Geographic. v.1-
[Anchorage, Alaska Geographic Society] 1972-
v. ill. (part col.). 23 x 31 cm.
Quarterly
Official publication of The Alaska Geographic Society.
Key title: Alaska geographic, ISSN 0361-1353.

1. Alaska — Description and travel — 1959-
—Periodicals. I. Alaska Geographic Society.

F901.A266   917.98'04'505   72-92087

Library of Congress   75[79112]   MARC-S

Cover: Focal point for Denali country, Mount McKinley, called Denali by many, rises 20,320 feet in the central Alaska Range. (Stu Pechek)

Previous page: The 20,320-foot summit of Mount McKinley towers above its neighbors in this view from Swan Lake on the south side of the Alaska Range. (Steve McCutcheon)

Facing page: Rani and Chlaus Lotscher row out of Home Lake on their way to the Tokositna River. The river runs from Tokositna Glacier to the Chulitna River northwest of Talkeetna. (Courtesy of Chlaus Lotscher)

STATEMENT OF OWNERSHIP MANAGEMENT and CIRCULATION

ALASKA GEOGRAPHIC is a quarterly publication, home office at P.O. Box 93370, Anchorage, AK 99509. Editor is Penny Rennick. Publisher is The Alaska Geographic Society, a nonprofit Alaska organization, P.O. Box 93370, Anchorage, AK 99509. Owners are Robert A. Henning and Phyllis G. Henning, P.O. Box 93370, Anchorage, AK 99509. Robert A. Henning and Phyllis G. Henning, husband and wife, are owners of 100 percent of all common stock outstanding.

ALASKA GEOGRAPHIC has a membership of 14,131.

I certify that the statement above is correct and complete.

ROBERT A. HENNING
Chief Editor

Table of Contents

Dear Members:

We will be beginning to make gradual changes in the content of your quarterly *ALASKA GEOGRAPHIC®*s starting with the next issue, *Kuskokwim*, the vast region that is represented by the basin of the Yukon River's companion river to the south.

Changes will be minimal at first, Letters to the Editor, Print North (book reviews and various worthy printed pickups), and eventually an exciting new adventure in a "pen pals" section we'll call "Sharing."

It will take some time to develop this one, but if it works it will be great. In this "Sharing" area, members will be encouraged to write to us, not in the accepted Letters to the Editor sense, but members writing to other members. We urge you to join in this one. In explanation, we want members to write about themselves, their family, what they do, their interests . . . and most important, a key element is that we want these letters backed up with photos of you and your family, etc. We want to be truly able to "see" each other and some hint of how we respectively live. Word limit should be two or three hundred words, but even a few dozen words can do the job if the picture support is good.

We'll hope for letters from all countries around the Polar Rim and our related North Pacific Rim. English is a pretty universal language, but we'll take on whatever translation problems we run into. The important thing is to begin a process of getting acquainted, each with each other . . . sort of a people to people geography. Knowing each other can at the same time teach us to better know each other's country . . . and to better know each other is to better understand each other. Good stuff. Join us.

Incidentally, at home here in Alaska, realize that "Sharing" will not all be Americans meeting Russians, or Japanese establishing correspondence with us, but there is need, and great value, in people in Kotzebue writing the people who live in Angoon, folks in Anchorage establishing letters and pictures contact with folks in Craig . . . Alaska is so doggone big, this or that region within Alaska may well be to the other much like a foreign country within one's own country. Tell us about you and yours. And for pictures, we'd like to have 35 millimeter positive color slides, but anything will do. Share.

Gradually, *ALASKA GEOGRAPHIC®* will cover many features in each issue, as opposed to the monographic approach we now employ. We aren't quitting the monographs. They will eventually be produced separately from the regular membership quarterly as books. Same format, same kind of beautiful full coverage in depth of a basic region or subject, but planned well in advance and treated as books, available to members along with their regular new quarterlies at deep discount. Two compelling

reasons dictate this change. The first is that in this manner we will be able to much better keep abreast of our changing times and to discuss with each other in greater depth and cohesiveness the many features and problems of the day that deserve thoughtful exploration too difficult for day-to-day newspapers

Russia, Japan, Korea, the Chinas, and elsewhere for us astride the Polar Rim and atop the Pacific Rim. It's an exciting new world out there and we are going to jump in and be a part of it. We are not talking about becoming "sort of a newspaper" or another general magazine. We're talking about top coverage by authoritative people and we also are talking about not only maintaining our reputation of today as "one of America's most beautiful magazines," but we'd like to instead become America's "THE most beautiful magazine."

Your suggestions will be appreciated.

Sincerely,

Robert A. Henning
President
The Alaska Geographic Society

P.S. Things are still very much "go" for our Hall of the North project at Alaska Pacific University in Anchorage. Some exciting new plans for that and we'll clue you in in more detail next issue.

In the meantime, mark "1991" on your calendar. We're going to do what we can to encourage throughout Alaska appropriate celebrations and recognition of our 250th Anniversary of Bering's landfall of the Alaska mainland in 1741.

to accomplish.

The other most compelling reason for the change is to make it possible for us to bring you an awful lot of wonderfully interesting and valuable editorial material that just isn't big enough, fat enough, long enough, to fill up a whole big issue all alone. As for variety,

Concentric ripples break the twilight stillness of a pond near Igloo Creek Campground in Denali National Park. (John Fowler)

and need for more resource related copy, there is plenty, both at home and "next door" with our neighbors. Things are beginning to open up with

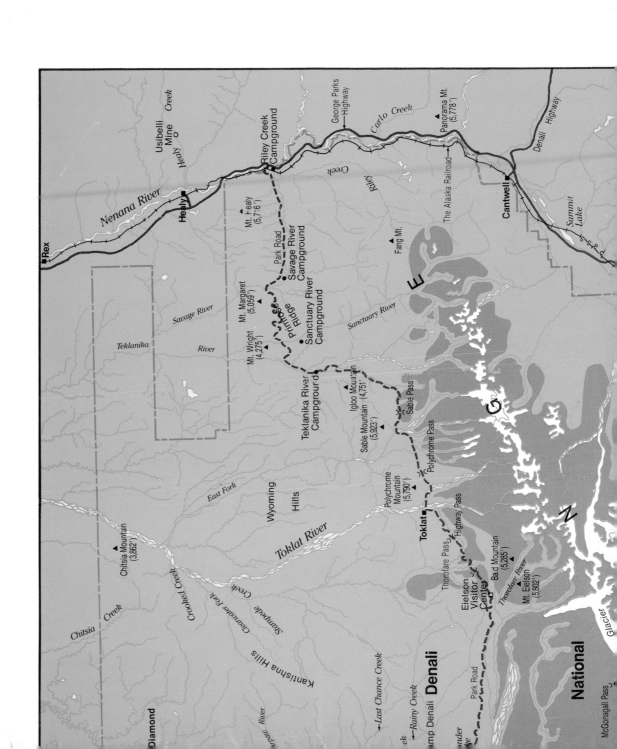

DENALI

Rex

Nenana River

Healy

Usibelli Mine

Healy Creek

Riley Creek Campground

George Parks Highway

Carlo Creek

Panorama Mt. (5,778')

Denali Highway

Cantwell

The Alaska Railroad

Summit Lake

A.R.R.

Mt. Fealy (5,7'6')

Park Road

Savage River Campground

Riley Creek

Fang Mt.

Mt. Margaret (5,059')

Primrose Ridge

Sanctuary River Campground

Sanctuary River

Savage River

River

Teklanika

Mt. Wright (4,275')

Teklanika River Campground

Igloo Mountain (4,751')

Sable Mountain (5,923')

Sable Pass

G

E

Chitsia Mountain (3,862')

East Fork

Wyoming Hills

Toklat River

Polychrome Mountain (5,790')

Polychrome Pass

Toklat

Highway Pass

N

Chitsia Creek

Crooked Creek

Clearwater Fork

Stampede Creek

Thorofare Pass

Eielson Visitor Center

Bad Mountain (5,285')

Thorofare River

Mt. Eielson (5,802')

Diamond

Kantishna Hills

Last Chance Creek

Rainy Creek

mp Denali

Park Road

Denali

National

Glacier

McGonagall Pass

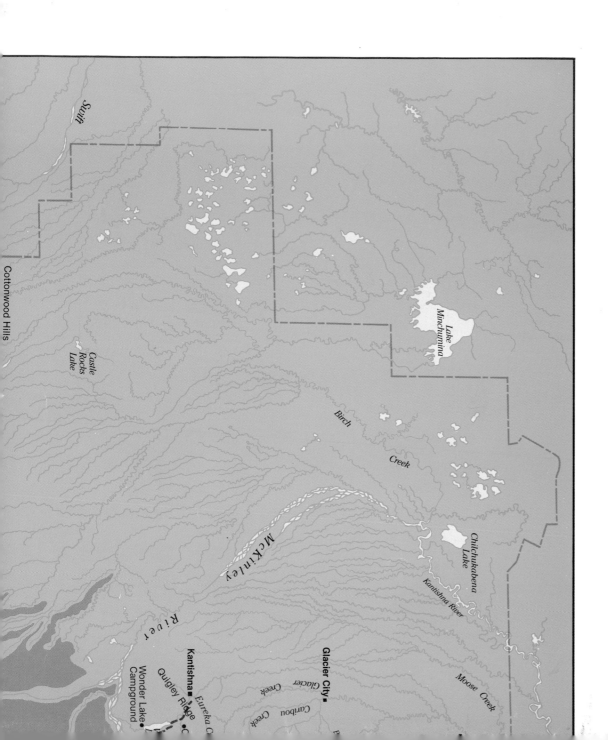
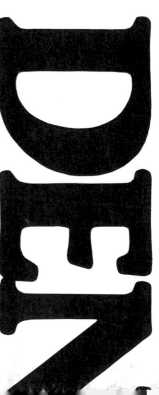

Denali Country

By Elaine Rhode

Editor's note: Anchorage resident Elaine Rhode is a freelance biologist and writer whose articles have appeared several times in *ALASKA GEOGRAPHIC*®.

If one place could epitomize all that is Alaska, that place would be Denali country, nearly dead center in the state and the heart of the last frontier. The highest mountain in North America and its surrounding state and national park-lands seem to capture the spirit, grandeur, wildness and abundance that Alaska brings to mind.

Denali country has become the destination of hundreds of thousands of

Byers Lake attracts the most visitors to Denali State Park. The lake is a short drive off the George Parks Highway and offers grayling, burbot, rainbow and whitefish for anglers. Two large campgrounds are nearby. (Brian Okonek)

visitors annually. The often-asked question is, "Have you seen *the* mountain yet?" Residents of Fairbanks and Anchorage, the two largest cities north and south of Denali country, judge the beauty of the day by whether *the* mountain is visible on the horizon. Unfortunately for the summer tourist, clear views of the 20,320-foot summit of Mount McKinley occur most often in winter. [**Editor's note:** Many people call the continent's tallest mountain Denali, but its official name remains Mount McKinley.]

Denali country is dominated by lofty, snow-covered peaks of the Alaska Range with Mount McKinley towering in their midst. To the north the landscape rolls across tundra and rises in low mountains called the Outer Range, then levels out in boggy muskeg and spruce forests laced by rivers. This land is Denali National Park and Preserve and is roadless except for a summer gravel road

running 91 miles west from the eastern boundary, then along the southern side of the Outer Range to the Kantishna mining district in the center of the park.

Northwest of a jagged line running from the Cottonwood Hills, past Castle Rocks Lake, and along Birch Creek and the Kantishna River lies one section of Denali National Preserve. The other section hangs off the southwestern corner of Denali country in the area southwest of Mount Russell and west of Chelatna Lake. [**Editor's note:** Lands within Denali National Park and Preserve fall into three categories: Pre-1980 Mount McKinley National Park lands have been designated wilderness. Territory added to the reserve in 1980 include both park additions and preserve additions. Sport hunting under state regulations is allowed in the preserve; subsistence hunting and trapping are permitted in park additions.]

Kim Blommel carries a backpack up a draw on Curry Ridge, a major topographic feature of Denali State Park. (Charlie Crangle)

To the southeast of the Alaska Range, three of McKinley's longest glaciers — Eldridge, Ruth and Tokositna — spill their meltwater into streams flowing toward the Pacific Ocean. Here Denali State Park commands a front row seat to the mountain spectacle and claims more summer viewing days than on the north side. Park rangers point out that even on cloudy days the weather will usually break near sunset and McKinley will show.

The George Parks Highway between Anchorage and Fairbanks runs through the state park, into a broad valley separating the Alaska Range from the Talkeetna Mountains and along the eastern boundary of the national park. Prior to the opening of this north-south highway in 1971, road access was only available seasonally from the east along the Denali Highway west from Paxson to Cantwell. The Alaska Railroad, on a route roughly paralleling the Parks Highway, continues its year-round service to Denali country begun in 1923.

The towns of Talkeetna, Cantwell and Healy serve visitors approaching the parks on the highway system. Talkeetna is also the air taxi center for flightseeing trips around the mountain and for glacier landings for climbers and skiers on the south side of the Alaska Range.

The name Denali comes from the Athabascans and means "the high one." According to legend, their forefathers witnessed the mountain's rise.

Yako, a strong, brave Indian, lived in a forested land where there were no women. On advice from Ses, the great bear, he built a canoe and floated westward down the Yukon River to ask Raven War Chief, Totson, for a wife from among his tribe's beautiful females.

A fisherman tries his luck for rainbow at Chelatna Lake, 42 miles northwest of Talkeetna. (Chlaus Lotscher)

Aspen and spruce give way to shrubs and finally to alpine tundra throughout Denali country. (Jim Shives)

As Yako reached the seashore, the wife of the second chief came to the beach offering her child, Tsukala, and warned Yako that Totson was preparing to kill him. Totson, a magician, brewed a storm to swamp Yako's canoe and whipped the waves higher with his magic paddle. Yako threw his war-quelling stone far ahead to calm the waters in his path, but waves still towered behind and to the sides.

In fury, Totson heaved his great war spear at Yako, but the brave saw it coming and changed the oncoming rear wave into a mountain of stone. The spear struck the summit and ricocheted skyward, touching the greatest wave coming from the opposite direction and, through Yako's magic, turning it into an even greater mountain of stone.

Totson's canoe crashed into the rear mountain, throwing him upon the rocks where he changed instantly into a large black bird, the Croaking Raven. Yako fell into exhausted sleep and when he awoke, he was in his beautiful forest with Tsukala, now a young woman, at his side. Looking back he saw the mountains he had created, "Denali, the high one," and "Sultana, his wife" (Mount Foraker).

Yako's waves of stone mingled with science recently when geologists working in Denali country pioneered new evidence that much of southern Alaska is a collage of terranes, exotic, deep-ocean-floor rocks formed in the tropics, broken away by faulting and carried northward by movement along great faults.

Geologists also found fossil fern leaves, reeds and impressions from tree trunks with lizardlike scales that grew 280 million years ago — but not on this continent.

It takes lots of imagination to see the tropics when looking at the snow-covered Alaska Range, but the fact that this raw, sharp land is still building is easier to comprehend. The traveling rock terranes bumped up against the ancient (350 million to 1 billion year-old) rocks of the Outer Range which once formed an older shore of North America. The newcomers slowly ground under that edge in the earth's crust or plate, contorting and creating heat enough to make molten, subterranean cores of granite that would eventually form

Mount Russell rises 11,670 feet in the southwest corner of the wilderness portion of Denali National Park. (Brian Okonek)

Mount McKinley and other peaks.

Running through Denali country today is this continent's longest weakness in the earth's crust, the Denali fault system. Longer than the well-known San Andreas fault in California, the Denali fault system can be traced with satellite imagery in a 900-mile arc from west near the Bering Sea to east into Canada and south toward Glacier Bay National Park in southeastern Alaska.

Some geologists believe it was movement along this fault system about two million years ago that finally shoved Mount McKinley and its neighbors skyward. The fault remains active. The 1912 eruption of Katmai volcano 350 miles to the southwest sent shock waves through the system destroying the climbing route of the 1910 Sourdough Expedition that allowed the trailblazers to go from 11,000 feet to McKinley's North Peak and back in one day.

Ironically, the mountains themselves are creating the erosional forces carving them away. Because of their great height, they catch and chill all moisture blowing in from the Gulf of Alaska to the south. Snow accumulates year-round above the 14,000-foot level, feeding scores of glaciers, six of which surrounding Mount McKinley are from 26 to 46 miles long. These gouge out or reduce to rubble everything in their path. During the Ice Age, glaciers spilled into the main park valley and sent meltwater through growing canyons in the Outer Range. Most of the land north of the range, however, was ice free.

Outcrops of chert, a sedimentary rock rich in silica, drew the earliest users

This panorama taken from Camp Denali on the north side of the Alaska Range shows Mount McKinley and its neighboring peaks. (Ed Scherockman; reprinted from A Tourist Guide to Mount McKinley *[1980])*

Mount Brooks, 11,940 feet

Mount Silverthrone, 13,200 feet

Mount Tatum, 11,140 feet

Mount Carpé, 12,550 feet
Mount Koven, 12,210 feet

South Peak of Mount McKinley, 20,320 feet (Main summit, two miles between South and North Peaks.)

North Peak of Mount McKinley, 19,470 feet

Browne Tower, 14,600 feet

Karstens Ridge, 11,000 to 14,000 feet

Wickersham Wall, over 14,000 feet vertical rise from base.

Windy Creek winds out of the Alaska Range to enter the Nenana River near Cantwell. (Penny Rennick, staff)

First autumn snow frosts Denali country. The first snow can come anytime from August on. National Park Service staff keep the park road open until about the second week in September. From then on, travelers using the road are on their own. (W.E. Ruth)

A beaver dam alters the flow of Windy Creek in the Alaska Range west of Cantwell. (George Wuerthner)

of Denali country. Prehistoric man quarried this easily flaked material to make hunting and skinning tools. An outcrop can be seen just southeast of Teklanika Campground on the park road. Most of the early use came from people living to the north and northwest of the Outer Range. The Alaska Range barred people from the south.

As unbelievable as it seems now, none of the early foreign explorers took much note of this continent's highest mountain. Focusing their attention on the coast in a quest for sea otter pelts or for the Northwest Passage to link Europe to the Orient, seldom did anyone venture inland. The first mention of "distant stupendous mountains covered with snow and apparently detached from one another" came in 1794 from English navigator Capt. George Vancouver, surveying Cook Inlet, about 130 miles south of the peaks.

Maps of Alaska's coastline grew in detail, but not until 1839 was a cluster of mountains depicted in the blank whiteness of the region's interior. Ironically, this Russian map, based on information collected by the governor of the Russian American Company, Baron Ferdinand von Wrangell, was supplanted by a map from the next Russian explorer, Lt. Laurenti Zagoskin, who did not approach the Denali region and therefore omitted the area from his map. Subsequent maps were based on Zagoskin's and continued to omit the mountains described by von Wrangell. Indeed, the official Russian map used in the sale of Alaska to the United States in 1867 left blank the entire arc of mountains.

A Dall sheep lamb considers its next step on the slopes of Igloo Mountain. Park visitors can usually see the world's only wild white sheep at Igloo, near Mount Wright above the Sanctuary River valley and on slopes above Nenana Canyon. (Alissa Crandall)

American explorer William H. Dall, carrying Zagoskin's map, traveled up the Yukon River in 1866 and named the mountains the Alaska Range, but did not single out McKinley for mention. Other explorers followed, some like Lt. Henry Allen of the U.S. Army, who saw the mountain from afar and was unimpressed by its height.

Two adventurous fur traders and prospectors, Alfred Mayo and Arthur Harper, navigated new territory up the Tanana River in 1878 and returned with news of gold on the river bars and of "a great ice mountain." Thirty-five years later, Harper's son Walter would be the first to reach the true summit of that ice mountain. But at the time, it was

the prospectors' tale of gold that lured more men toward the Interior. Prospector Frank Densmore, however, was so impressed by the huge mountain he saw in 1889 from Lake Minchumina that he could talk of nothing else and soon gold seekers began calling it "Densmore's Mountain."

Another prospector, William Dickey from New Hampshire, changed the nation's attitude toward the mountain. While he and a companion prospected up the Susitna River in 1896, they came in full view of the Alaska Range and "Densmore's Mountain." With remarkable accuracy, Dickey estimated its height to be more than 20,000 feet. Returning to the States, he wrote an article for the New York *Sun* newspaper and *National Geographic* magazine saying, "We have no doubt that this peak is the highest in North America." Until then, everyone thought that 18,008-foot Mount St. Elias near the Gulf of Alaska coast on the Alaska-Yukon Territory border was the continent's highest mountain.

The name he hung on the mountain was chosen more for spite than for reverence. During his trip he had spent many weary hours with two prospectors who loudly boosted the merits of free silver for backing the U.S. Treasury. In retaliation, Dickey dubbed the mountain after the champion of the gold standard, Gov. William McKinley of Ohio who would soon be elected the nation's 25th president. Two years later, the 17,400-foot mountain just west of Mount McKinley, referred to locally as "Denali's wife," would be named Mount

13

South Side Development

The beauty of the area to the south of Denali has long been appreciated; in fact, artist Sydney Laurence painted some of his most famous views of Mount McKinley from a knoll above the Tokositna River. Because of this beauty and the area's proximity to the road system, it is a natural choice for a visitor/recreation center, an idea that has been talked about and studied for many years.

In 1951 Bradford Washburn, climber, photographer and scientist who first mapped McKinley, proposed a recreational facility in the Tokositna area, about 15 miles west of the Parks Highway in present-day Denali State Park. More recent interest in this area has included its mention in the 1969 Mount McKinley National Park master plan and a 1978 Alaska Division of Parks-National Park Service study evaluating Tokositna's development potential.

After Washburn's proposal, the next major movement toward development on McKinley's south side came in 1968, when the Alaska Department of Economic Development's study on ways to increase tourism in Alaska suggested the need for a hotel complex in the area.

One of the proposed locations was the Indian Ridge Site, one mile east of the Parks Highway near Chulitna Pass. A 300-room hotel/lodge was to be located on the ridge at the 1,700-foot level.

The following year, the National Park Service studied locations for a tourist complex, selecting a spot on state land on the south end of Curry Ridge, along the Parks Highway near the southern boundary of present-day Denali State Park. The site was chosen in part for its superlative view of McKinley and surrounding peaks. This study helped encourage the legislature to create the state park in 1970.

In 1972 the new George Parks Highway between Anchorage and Fairbanks brought visitors in numbers never before seen to the more easily accessible state and national parks. Then, in the mid-1970s, talk of moving the capital from Juneau to a location between Anchorage and Fairbanks raised the possibility of an increased population base within reach of the parks, resulting in a corresponding increase in recreational demand.

These factors led to several proposals for development in the McKinley area. In a 1973 report to the Land Use Planning Commission of Alaska, developers unveiled an ambitious plan for an all-season recreational and resort complex, privately financed but with possible state and federal grants for major public facilities. The complex was to be located near Ramsdyke Creek, in the Tokositna area Bradford Washburn had touted 20 years earlier. The project

A hiker surveys the majesty of Tokositna Glacier and Mount McKinley from Denali State Park. The glacier begins east of Mount Hunter and extends southeast for 23 miles. This area is one of the proposed sites for a visitor center on the south side of the Alaska Range. (Brian Okonek)

For decades, major access to the south side has been along the Petersville Road, an approximately 40-mile route originally blazed to supply miners and homesteaders in the area. (Pete Martin)

took on immense proportions, with talk at one point of suspending a Teflon-covered dome over the complex to control the climate. Proposed year-round indoor and outdoor activities included swimming, horseback riding, tobogganing, golf, curling and square dancing. There was also to be a creativity center, offering a symphony and artists in residence. Although the scheme generated a great deal of public interest and a deluge of reports, opposition to the type and scale of the plan was widespread. There was also an undercurrent of concern about mining claims adja-

cent to the area, and the overall cost of building a road to the site seemed prohibitive. The plan was shelved when funding could not be obtained for further phases of the project.

In 1974 an Alaska Division of Parks study concluded that the Byers Lake area was the best site for a lodge, visitor center and ski area; the proposal was discussed in more detail in the 1975 master plan for Denali State Park. The lake's easy access from the Parks Highway and diverse recreational opportunities did ultimately lead to development of a campground, picnic sites, boat launch and small boat-in campground there.

The National Park Service's general management plan for Denali National Park, completed in 1984, cited the need for relief from overcrowding of existing tourist facilities in the park, and looked to Denali State Park for that relief. With this in mind, state and federal agencies began a study of the "South Denali Visitor Complex" on Curry Ridge including a visitor's center, lodge and ski area. The site, near the Parks Highway and Alaska Railroad, offered spectacular views of McKinley, and the varied environment made possible a wide range of year-round outdoor activities.

A formal proposal for the Curry Ridge site was prepared in

1986, but resulting public concern led to yet another study, outlined in the Denali State Park Master Plan Update (March 1988). The first phase of that study — a regional analysis — had been completed by early 1988, in preparation for public meetings in May of that year. Subsequent phases, all dependent on legislative funding, include identification of site criteria, testing of criteria to select a site, environmental impact statement and a detailed site analysis. The final step would involve working with the private sector to find investors for privately owned recreational facilities. According to the Alaska Division of Parks, the project probably could not be completed before 1992 or 1993.

Miners followed early explorers to the south side of Denali. Today mining, such as at this camp in the Peters Hills, and bush living still generate the most activity in this area. (Pete Martin)

23

Measuring Mountains

By Kim Heacox

Editor's note: A former ranger at Denali National Park, Kim is now a freelance writer and photographer living in Anchorage.

Robert Muldrow, a topographer on the 1898 U.S. Geological Survey expedition into Interior Alaska, carried on his back a heavy wooden box that one might have thought contained gold or dynamite, given the way Muldrow handled it. Instead, it contained a high resolution telescope — called a theodolite — used to measure horizontal and vertical angles from great distances. It was the indisputable state-of-the-art instrument for measuring mountains.

Two years earlier, William Dickey — a prospector who named Mount McKinley for the Ohio governor running for president — had estimated the summit of the mountain at more than 20,000 feet. It sounded more like fiction than fact to a professional man of maps like Muldrow. Could McKinley really be that high? The highest mountain in North America? Muldrow, a scientist who prided himself on precision, aimed to find out. Several times as his party made camp along the Susitna and Tanana

Mount McKinley looms over Anchorage, about 150 miles to the south.
(Myron Wright)

rivers, Muldrow trudged up ridges that afforded clear views of the mountain, set up his theodolite and sighted in on the summit which at times was nearly 100 miles away. It wasn't easy.

The science of measuring mountains had been, and still is, an extremely difficult task. Many a surveyor before Muldrow, especially those in the Himalayas, had seen their reputations tumble after proclaiming the precise elevation of some summit, which later turned out to be not-so-precise. One surveyor wrote, "... the calculation of the heights of Himalayan peaks is a realm of such erudite complexity that not even angels armed with theodolites and plumblines would dare to tread therein."

To calculate a mountain's elevation using a theodolite, a surveyor must shoot the angle of the peak's rise from at least two different locations, each of which has a known elevation. Having measured the distance between the two theodolite stations, he knows the dimensions of two angles and one side of a huge imaginary triangle delineated by the mountain's summit and the stations. He plugs these numbers into a trigonometric formula, corrects for the curve of the earth, and arrives at the elevation of the mountain.

But there are problems. First, if the computed heights of the theo-dolite stations are wrong, everything else will be wrong. Second, atmospheric refraction — the tendency of light rays to bend as they pass through the atmosphere between mountain and surveyor — causes the summit to appear higher than it is. The precise amount of refraction depends on the air temperature and density, which can change dramatically in hours. From sunrise to noon, for example, as the air warms up and the refraction properties shift, the triangulated elevation of a distant peak will "shrink" several hundred feet. The effect of this warp factor increases exponentially with every mile between surveyor and mountain. Some triangulated elevations of the tallest Himalayan peaks, shot with theodolites from the plains of India, have been adjusted nearly 1,400 feet to compensate for estimated refraction. And third, plumbline deflection — the tendency for an immense mass of mountains, like the Alaska Range, to pull the leveling bubbles in a theodolite slightly away from the earth's center of gravity — can ruin a surveyor's accuracy. Mass has its own gravity in addition to the earth's gravity. If the landscape to one side of a measurement station is flat, while terrain in the other direction slopes upward, i.e. has more mass, the plumbline pointing to the center of the earth will be thrown off. This discrepancy is unimportant over a short distance, but substantially affects measurements taken 100 miles or more away from the mountain's summit.

When Robert Muldrow aimed his theodolite at Mount McKinley, the odds for success were against him. His results: 20,464 feet. The actual summit elevation, determined later by more precise and sophisticated theodolite measurements and aerial studies, is 20,320 feet. Muldrow was 144 feet too high — an error of only 0.7 percent — probably due to atmospheric refraction. Despite missing the mark, it was an admirable attempt back in 1898.

Even today the elevations of some of the world's highest mountains remain debatable, as well as the methods used to measure them. In 1987 a series of combined measurements in the Himalayas suggested that K2, long thought to be the second highest mountain in the world next to Everest, might indeed be the highest. But in 1988, sophisticated measurements by four Navstar satellites high above the Himalayas not only confirmed Everest as the king of mountains (about 800 feet higher than K2), but measured both peaks to within inches of their exact altitudes. Things have changed considerably since 1898; Robert Muldrow would be astounded.

range exhibited itself from Denali to the sea. To the right hand the glittering, tiny threads of streams draining the mountain range into the Chulitna and Sushitna Rivers, and so to Cook's Inlet and the Pacific Ocean, spread themselves out; to the left the affluents of the Kantishna and the Nenana drained the range into the Yukon and Bering Sea.

Yet the chief impression was not of our connection with the earth so far below, its rivers and its seas, but rather of detachment from it. We seemed alone upon a dead world, as dead as the mountains on the moon. Only once before can the writer remember a similar feeling of being neither in the world or of the world, and that was at the bottom of the Grand Canyon of the Colorado, in Arizona, its savage granite walls as dead as this savage peak of ice.

Above us the sky took a blue so deep that none of us had ever gazed upon a midday sky like it before. It was a deep, rich, lustrous, transparent blue, as dark as a Prussian blue, but intensely blue. . . . We first noticed the darkening tint of the upper sky in the Grand Basin, and it deepened as we rose. . . .

It is difficult to describe at all the scene which the top of the mountain presented. One was not occupied with the thought of description but wholly possessed with the breadth and glory of it. . . . Yet we could not linger, . . . the miserable limitations of the flesh gave us continual warning to depart; we grew colder and still more wretchedly cold. The thermometer stood at 7° in the full sunshine, and the north wind was keener than ever. My fingers were so cold that I would not venture to withdraw them from the mittens to change the film in the camera, and the other men were in like case; indeed, our hands were by this time so numb as to make it almost impossible to operate a camera at all. A number of photographs had been taken, though not half we should have liked to take, but it is probable that, however many more exposures had been made, they would have been little better than those we got. Our top-of-the-mountain photography was a great disappointment. One thing we learned: exposures at such altitude should be longer than those below, perhaps owing to the darkness of the sky.

When the mercurial barometer had been read the tent was thrown down and abandoned, the first of the series of abandonments that marked our descent from the mountain. The tent-pole was used for a moment as a flagstaff while Tatum hoisted a little United States flag he had patiently and skillfully constructed in our camps below out of two silk handkerchiefs and the cover of a sewing-bag. Then the pole was put to its permanent use. It had already been carved with a suitable inscription, and now a transverse piece, already prepared and fitted, was lashed securely to it and it was planted on one of the little snow turrets of the summit — the sign of our redemption, high above North America. Only some peaks in the Andes and some peaks in the Himalayas rise above it in all the world. It was of light, dry birch and, though six feet in length, so slender that we think it may weather many a gale. And Walter thrust it into the

36

"I remember no day in my life so full of toil, distress, and exhaustion, and yet so full of happiness and keen gratification."
                                        —Hudson Stuck

(Photo by John Fowler)

snow so firmly at a blow that it could not be withdrawn again. . . .

It was 1:30 p.m. when we reached the summit and two minutes past three when we left; yet so quickly had the time flown that we could not believe we had been an hour and a half on top. The journey down was a long, weary grind. . . .

A thermometer reading to 100° below zero, left at this spot, would, in my judgment, perhaps yield a lower minimum than had ever yet been authentically recorded on earth. . . . I did not leave my own alcohol minimum — scaled to 95° below zero, and yielding, by estimation, perhaps ten degrees below the scaling — there, because of the difficulty of giving explicit directions that should lead to its ready recovery, and at the close of such a day of toil as is involved in reaching the summit, men have no stomach for prolonged search. . . .

However, for one, the writer was largely unconscious of weariness in that descent. All the way down, my thoughts were occupied with the glorious scene my eyes had gazed upon and should gaze upon never again. In all human probability I would never climb that mountain again; yet if I climbed it a score more times I would never be likely to repeat such vision. . . .

We reached our eighteen-thousand-foot camp about five o'clock, a weary but happy crew. It was written in the diary that night: "I remember no day in my life so full of toil, distress, and exhaustion, and yet so full of happiness and keen gratification."

Climbing Denali

By Karen Jettmar

Editor's note: A former teacher, Karen now works for The Wilderness Society in Anchorage.

In 1973, I got my first clear view of Mount McKinley from my land in the Talkeetna foothills. The first rays of the morning sun struck the summit peak as I gazed in wonder. As I walked on a ridge-top trail towards the mountain, it grew and grew until it hardly seemed real, the way it touched the sky. I knew then one day I would attempt to climb it.

Ten years later, Denali beckoned still. All winter long I had gazed out at the mountains that surrounded my small cabin in Southeast Alaska. Yakutat, with

Karen Jettmar rests for a moment on a 16,000-foot notch on the West Buttress route to McKinley's summit. (Courtesy of Karen Jettmar)

its breathtaking views of the St. Elias and Fairweather mountain ranges, was an inspirational setting from which to plan such an expedition. I made tentative plans to climb with friends who lived scattered across Alaska. Come May, other commitments arose and before long I was the only remaining member of our team. Undaunted, I decided the time was still right to climb "The High One." I would find a group to join, or go solo, if necessary.

During the previous summer I had made numerous trips into the St. Elias Range with National Park Service ranger Clarence Summers. Now my training consisted mainly of long runs along wave-swept beaches and logging roads. By mid-May, I'd organized my ski and climbing gear. I sewed extra stuffsacks, a pair of overboots and a vapor barrier sack for inside my sleeping bag, and added them to the mountain of gear which grew in a corner closet. There

remained only a couple of weeks of school at Yakutat Elementary where I was a teacher. I made food lists and put together a menu for 24 days on the mountain. At high altitudes, the body craves carbohydrates; proteins are hard to digest. As a vegetarian, I eat mostly carbohydrates anyway, so it was easy to plan meals. I selected fast-cooking brown rice, rolled oats and other hot cereals, hot drinks, dried soups, dehydrated potatoes, homemade pancake mix, freeze-dried vegetables, bagels, cheese, granola, dried fruit, fig bars, honey, nuts, homemade cookies and sourdough bread, packing it in three-day food sacks. I baked a huge pan of Logan Bread — a dense loaf developed for ascents of Canada's Mount Logan — which contains just about everything. My recipe book claimed, "A two-by-two-inch square will sustain a man for a day." I figured it could sustain a woman, too.

School ended and I flew to Anchorage. On June 4th, I boarded the Alaska Railroad for Talkeetna. A party atmosphere filled my train car; there were three other expedition groups on their way to Mount McKinley.

In Talkeetna, there was no shortage of climbers. This tiny town in the upper Susitna Valley bustles with mountaineers each spring. I quickly caught the infectious spirit of the community, as climbers flew in and out of the mountains, and news of groups on various routes spread by word of mouth. Kevin Slater and Paul Spanjer, Outward Bound instructors from Maine and Colorado, invited me to join their team.

June 5th dawned sunny and clear. Our afternoon flight with K2 Aviation confirmed, I took a final inventory of my food and equipment, threw out a few superfluous items, then ran over to the trading post for a jar of peanut butter. Later, in the noon heat, I abandoned my shorts and donned heavy long underwear and double climbing boots. Soon, we were taxiing on the gravel strip, then were airborne and soaring over the Talkeetna, Susitna and Chulitna rivers. Foothills gave way to snow-clad ridges, granite walls and sinuous glaciers. Pilot Jim Okonek landed on the southeast fork of Kahiltna Glacier, just outside Denali National Park. Spindrift from the prop blast settled to reveal ridges rising cathedrallike from the glacier. I could hardly believe I was finally there, mentally and physically prepared to climb North America's highest peak.

Frances Randall, Fairbanks concert pianist and Kahiltna Base Camp radio

operator, also known as the caretaker of the "Kahiltna Hilton," greeted us with a friendly smile. (Frances is gone now. After spending about 10 seasons on the mountain, she passed away in 1984.) Minutes later, pilot Lowell Thomas Jr. landed with a reporter from *USA Today*. Jim took off, his plane quickly becoming a tiny speck against mountain walls. Scattered about Kahiltna Base, other climbing groups were in various stages of arrival or departure. Paul, Kevin and I rigged up harnesses for our plastic sleds, roped up and attached skins (mohair strips which prevent slipping) to our skis before putting them on. Then we skied a short downhill run to the main fork of Kahiltna Glacier.

Prospective challengers of Mount McKinley construct a tent frame at Kahiltna Base Camp on Kahiltna Glacier. (Karen Jettmar)

We followed the east side of the 2-mile-wide glacier, skirting large crevasses as we glided, or rather plodded, our way north. This was my first time pulling a sled on a climb, and it felt great. I chose to climb alpine-style as much as possible, carrying everything in a single push. For a few days, this meant moving 80 to 90 pounds of gear up the glacier. Using a sled, I could load the heaviest items onto it and lighten my backpack. This way my shoulders wouldn't bear the burden of the load. Clouds crept up from the south and by evening it was snowing. The temperature felt fairly warm, perhaps 25 degrees.

We stopped for the night at 7,500 feet, after six and a half hours of travel. Paul dug a shallow pit for the tents, while Kevin and I fashioned crude walls. Snow ledges around the tents provided a measure of protection for our flimsy nylon shelters in the ever-present possibility of wind. After dinner, crawling into my down bag at 12:30 a.m., it was still light outside. I worried a bit about snow and wind and prayed for good weather for the next couple of weeks. Our route, the West Buttress, has been called a "walk-up." I have too much respect for Alaska's mountains to take such a cavalier attitude. People have died on this route.

In the morning, the glacier sparkled with a layer of new snow and the clouds had disappeared. It was astonishingly clear. Even the wind had died. Inside the tent, it felt like a greenhouse. Arising and packing were a pleasure in such warmth. I smeared my face and lips with 20-factor sunblock, draped a bandana over my head and neck and donned a baseball cap and glacier sunglasses, all to protect myself from the sun's ultraviolet rays. After a breakfast of hot cereal and dried fruit, we set out. With skins on our skis, we could ski up the gradual incline of Kahiltna without slipping. The trail was well-marked with wands to avoid the crevasses. We instinctively settled into a rhythm and pace which allowed us to

A willing heart can often overcome physical handicaps, enabling this group of disabled mountaineers from Challenge Alaska to enjoy a trip on Ruth Glacier. (John Fowler)

Mount Dan Beard provides the backdrop as Pam Robinson checks the mail at the landing strip in the Don Sheldon Amphitheater on Ruth Glacier. At least 10 routes up the East and South Buttresses and the Southeast Spur to McKinley's summit leave from Ruth Glacier. (Charlie Crangle)

maintain comfortable tension on the rope, and no one felt pressured to ski too fast. By noon, the surface of the snow had softened and we were slogging along. The sky was cobalt blue, the mountains crystalline. There was nowhere else on earth I wanted to be.

We approached a guided expedition led by John Svenson. By now, the sun was shining fiercely, making the glacier seem like a summer beach. It was definitely T-shirt weather. John and others had gone a step further. They were sprawled out, shirts off, drinking beer and listening to rock and roll music on a tapedeck with external speakers. This group was obviously traveling with more baggage than we were hauling. They carried their gear in stages, caching supplies at a higher altitude each day, returning to sleep at a lower altitude, then hauling a second load the following day. This expedition-style climbing allows for more acclimatization, and increases the risk of hitting bad weather because more time is spent on the mountain than during an alpine-style climb of the same route.

Basking here in the hot sun, sharing lunch and stories, we found it hard to believe Denali is one of the coldest mountains in the world. After a long break, we continued up Kahiltna, stopping for the day at about 9,000 feet. We dug a pit for the tents and prepared a hearty supper. So far, my food selection seemed excellent and I felt great. In the crystal-clear sky, the peaks surrounding us were resplendent. Snug once again in my tent, I wondered what the climb had been like for Dr. Bradford Washburn,

pioneer of the West Buttress route in 1951 with William Hackett and James Gale. Up to that time, Denali had only been successfully climbed by about 30 people. In 1969, a friend of mine was part of the 65th successful ascent. As we slept that night, there were probably more than 65 parties on the mountain. Times have certainly changed. Now 500 or more people attempt the West Buttress route and 100 or 200 try more difficult routes each year. Less than half make it to the summit.

June 7th was another unbelievably clear day. We pulled our sleds to 10,000 feet. Here, where the glacier narrowed slightly, I began to see many abandoned tent sites and frequent yellow stains on the glacier. Two rules for good health on the mountain are: 1) don't collect yellow snow for drinking purposes and, 2) drink water prodigiously. With all the time it takes to melt enough snow for the water our bodies needed, an hour or two went into food preparation morning and evening. The park service has insisted on a stringent program of waste disposal on the mountain. Naturally, we carried all our trash back to Talkeetna. In the case of solid human wastes, we used plastic garbage sacks, then deposited the bags into deep crevasses. It was important for us to minimize our impact.

We reached our first major hill, known by some climbers as Squirrel Hill. We reorganized our gear and left sleds and skis behind, buried and marked with wands. Steeper climbing and stronger winds made it safer to wear crampons. I started up the steep slope with an enormous pack. My heart pounded. At 11,000 feet? Ridiculous! I jettisoned gear, putting it into stuffsacks, burying and marking them well. It would be tragic to return and not be able to locate essential food, fuel and clothing.

With a manageable pack, we continued to about 12,000 feet, excavating two old tent sites. My slight headache disappeared after several hot drinks; the liquid soothed my dry throat. We ate dinner with the peaks of Foraker and Hunter rising southwest of us, Peters Glacier and the green tundra drifting off to the northwest. To the east, above us, a smooth lenticular cloud sat atop the summit of McKinley; it looked distant and cold. Bushed, I crawled into my bag at 9 p.m., with the sun still high in the western sky.

June 8th was another clear day. With crampons strapped on our boots, we ascended a broad, windswept plateau and turned southeast toward Windy Corner. Our progress had been good. For me, the reward was a view that became more magnificent the higher I went. We followed a shallow notch along the flanks of the West Buttress and climbed around the corner. The snow was hard, with good footing. Huge crevasses shattered the icefields below us and mammoth blocks of ice lay scattered about. I worried about an avalanche. We continued to hug the foot of the West Buttress and reached the 14,200-foot basin by afternoon. Four climbers on their way down offered us a bag of food. One fellow had taken his glove off on the summit for 30 seconds and got frostbite. Sobering. We dove into the food, gorging ourselves on onion bagels, date-oatmeal cookies, cheese and crackers.

We planned to stay at 14,200 feet for a few nights to acclimatize, so we carefully selected a safe, comfortable campsite. I dug down through a soft, fluffy layer and found solid, chunky snow perfect for cutting blocks for a protective wall. I cut large rectangular blocks with a snow saw, and we piled them bricklike around the tents until they were no longer visible. Out of the wind, I fashioned an entryway. Finally, we carved out tabletops for our kitchen and collected snow in stuffsacks. The well-stocked mountain kitchen always has a supply of snow ready for melting.

This morning there was not a cloud in the sky, not a breath of wind to disturb a single crystal of snow. The weather was remarkable! My tent was like a sauna, thankfully, for I felt terrible. Around my eyes and at the base of my scalp, my head ached. I had no motivation, no thirst, no hunger; I simply felt debilitated. I forced myself to fire up my stove to melt snow. I knew I needed to drink fluids. After several cups of hot tea, I forced myself to eat a piece of bread and immediately felt nauseous. All day I lay inside the tent, only mustering the energy to complete one constructive project — laundering my lightweight long underwear. It stiffened like a board after I rinsed it in warm water, then eventually dried under the sun's warming rays. I tried to read, but mostly just rolled around, feeling listless and unmotivated, dozing off and on. I thought, "Why am I here?" In the evening, disconsolate, I forced myself to eat a handful of granola and some hot soup. Later, I

Blocks of snow make perfect tables and shelves for climbers on Mount McKinley.
(Karen Jettmar)

almost vomited. I knew why I felt bad — it was the altitude. Perhaps I should have slept lower last night.

Our fifth completely clear day in a row dawned. I felt great today. Paul and Kevin decided they would attempt the West Rib, a route which is a bit more difficult and would take more time. I decided to continue on the West Buttress. We wished each other good luck as they went off to cache some gear and I set out to explore the plateau. There were about

43

25 climbers there now. Acknowledging that this route is no wilderness experience because of the number of people on it at any one time, part of the fun came from socializing in an international climbing community. There were climbers from the U.S., France, Germany, Spain, Canada and Japan. The park ranger informed me he brought 19-year-old climber Rolf Grange down the rescue gully from 17,500 feet to the basin last night. Rolf and partner Brian Becker met avalanches while climbing a new route on Cassin Ridge. In their struggles, Rolf's feet were frostbitten; Lowell Thomas was on his way to pick him up. A dozen of us worked together stamping out an airstrip, the highest in North America for a fixed-wing plane. With impeccable *savoir faire*, Lowell bounded from his plane on skis and schussed downslope carrying a couple of sprigs of spruce and a wild rose. How sweet and pungent their aroma in this sterile world of ice, rock and snow.

During the next couple of days, I descended to 12,000 feet to retrieve gear and ascended the headwall looming above camp to cache gear and acclimatize. The stretch from the basin to the crest of the headwall at 16,100 feet is the steepest part of the climb. With a constant 45-degree slope, this section requires concentrated effort. Standing in the shadow of the towering wall of ice, I attached a jumar ascender — a special gripper usually used only in emer-

With the goal nearly at hand, a climber follows the summit ridge to the 20,320-foot top of the South Peak of McKinley, the continent's highest point. (Charlie Crangle)

gencies, but which I chose for added protection while climbing alone — to the fixed line. I planted my ice axe firmly into the slope, then kicked the front points of my crampons in hard as I climbed. Two hours later, I reached the top of the ridge. Majestic peaks rose abruptly and sharply in all directions. Crevasses below camp reminded me of wrinkles on aged skin. On the mountain's frozen vastness, a climbing party moving across the basin was a mere line of dark specks linked together by an imaginary thread. I felt humbled by my surroundings.

A Japanese party of eight climbers met with misfortune. Another rescue — several climbers from the High Altitude Research Camp brought two of the climbers down from 17,200 feet. One had broken ribs; another had a broken arm; three others were sick with pulmonary edema.

Two climbers from California, Steve and Paul, hosted a party in the evening; seven of us piled into a huge dome tent and shared stories, food and hot drinks. At midnight, I stepped outside again. In the dying sunlight, sculpted ridges reflected a delicate pink light. My thermometer registered 27 degrees below zero.

The following day, after a full morning of activities (which included observing the turbo-jet evacuation of the Japanese party and undergoing various physiological tests at the medical research camp with Dr. Peter Hackett), I ascended the headwall once more, this time with Minnesotans Tim and Ann. On the crest, I located yesterday's cache, carefully buried to prevent ravens from pilfering it. We climbed another couple hundred feet, then dug protected tent sites into the side of the narrow ridge at 16,400 feet. A layer of clouds covered the lower glaciers once more. Above us, a high haze swept over the sun, and wind blew snow over the summit. A storm was on the way.

It snowed and blew all night

This view shows McKinley from the gateway of the Great Gorge of Ruth Glacier. (Bradford Washburn, reprinted from A Tourist Guide to Mount McKinley)

long; every hour or so we yelled out to each other over the howl of the wind and loud flapping of our tents. In this manner, we took turns going outside to shovel snow from around the tent. Heavy snowfall could bury us. In the flat light, with blowing snow obscuring my vision, up and down were barely distinguishable.

In the morning, it was still snowing. We slept in until 11:30. After digging out most of the snow accumulated around the tent and laying articles of clothing out to dry, the wind suddenly lashed out and blew snow all over everything again. We ate, read, nursed our chapped faces and shoveled snow all day.

The following day, it was still snowing hard. I finished my novel; the other was cached at 11,000 feet. I began to feel restless, even with hourly snow shoveling. Ann and Tim were deep into long novels. I couldn't persuade either one to loan me theirs, even with a bribe of chocolate chip cookies. Late in the afternoon, Steve and German climber Detlev stopped by on their way down from 17,200 feet to retrieve a cache. They invited me to join them for the climb back up. Snow swirled around as I hurriedly packed up. Miraculously, we climbed right out of the snowstorm into bright sunshine. We threaded a path through granite boulders and over a narrow ridge that dropped off thousands of feet on either side, to emerge onto a plateau at 17,230 feet. In a frenzy, we pitched our three tents and quickly cut snow blocks for walls. It was another cold night — 35 degrees below zero.

June 16th, summit day, dawned clear and cold. While my pressurized

A 3,000-foot cliff rises at McKinley's 17,350-foot level with a view of Mount Foraker in the background. (Bradford Washburn, reprinted from A Tourist Guide to Mount McKinley)

stove roared outside the tent, I carefully dressed in long underwear and pile pants, wind pants, vapor barrier sock liners and double socks, pile jacket, down parka, wool balaclava, pile hat, sunglasses, double mitts, overboots and crampons. I packed an extra parka, down mittens and other extra mitts, goggles, down pants, a sleeping pad, stove and fuel, food and a liter of water. A wild, anticipatory feeling flowed through my being, as I considered the final challenge before me. After a hearty breakfast, Detlev, Thomas (who had joined us at 14,200 feet), Steve, Paul and I set out. At Denali Pass, 18,200 feet, we switched lead positions and stopped for a snack. The sky began to fill with wispy cirrus clouds. It was very cold. My drinking water started turning to ice crystals. Though the summit was less than 2,200 feet above, miles still separated us from it.

We spread out across a broad plateau, passing west of Archdeacon's Tower, each following our own pace, alone in our thoughts. In the midst of swirling clouds, icy blasts of wind lashed out, and I hoped I would stay warm. At the headwall, rising from 19,600 feet, progress was snaillike. We plowed through knee-deep snow, gasping for air. I felt like I was running a marathon with lead weights on my feet, and slid back downslope half a step for each two steps I took. I alternately froze and roasted, as the wind blew or died, and the sun infrequently popped out from the clouds. I felt lightheaded, slightly nauseous and terribly thirsty. I'd never felt this tired in my life. All my energy and concentration went into lifting my legs and my ice axe. Atop the summit ridge, I could see Detlev and Thomas on the summit. Only a couple hundred feet to go.

Finally, I reached the top. Enveloped in a cloud of ice crystals, I could see very little, save the summit ridge of McKinley's North Peak. A poem I once read came to mind:

You never conquer a mountain
You stand on the summit a moment
Then the wind blows your
    footprints away.

In the bitter cold, I took a few deep breaths and began my descent. The climb had been worth every moment of the effort.

47

So You Want To Climb McKinley . . .

Climbers contemplating a trek to the summit of Mount McKinley need to make extensive plans, carefully considering seemingly ordinary factors such as how to get there and what to take. To help, the National Park Service offers general information for climbers in a booklet called *Mountaineering.* Copies may be requested from the park service at the address below. Following are some basic guidelines outlined in the booklet.

There are three mandatory requirements of anyone attempting to climb McKinley:
1) The expedition leader must register with the mountaineering ranger before the start of the climb, preferably two to six months in advance;
2) Expeditions must check in and out at the beginning and end of their climbs at the Talkeetna Ranger Station;
3) Waste generated by climbing parties must be packed out; human waste should be collected and dumped into a deep crevasse.

Regulations require climbs to begin at the park boundary; air drops inside the park are prohib-ited. Parties should have at least four members, as larger parties provide greater strength and self-rescue capability. Although several solo ascents have been completed, solo travel is discouraged.

Snow conditions and weather for climbing McKinley are usually best from early May through early July. By August there is more inclement weather with heavier snowfall, and melting snow bridges over crevasses make travel on the lower glaciers more difficult.

The most frequently climbed routes on Mount McKinley are the West Buttress (used by about three-quarters of all climbers), South Face and Muldrow Glacier. Access from the south is by ski plane from Talkeetna to the Southeast Fork of Kahiltna Glacier or other glaciers on the south side of McKinley. From the north, the most common access is an 18- to 20-mile cross-country route by foot, skis or dogsled from Wonder Lake.

Properly outfitting a climbing expedition is essential to its success. Meals should be planned carefully, including enough food to provide 4,000 to 5,000 calories per person

Protected behind walls made of snow blocks, climbers set up camp at the 17,200-foot level of McKinley's West Buttress. (Bill Sherwonit)

per day for the expected duration of the climb (about two and one-half to three and one-half weeks for the West Buttress route), plus a large reserve for emergencies. Food should be repackaged before the trip to eliminate as much garbage as possible. Clothing should be adequate for the severest arctic conditions, including a down parka and pants, wind parka and pants, wool socks, face mask, sun hat, and both light gloves and long-sleeved insulated mittens. A group's other equipment and supplies might include: boots adequate for preventing frostbite; snowshoes or skis; stoves, extra stove parts for repairs and plenty of fuel; ice axes; crampons; snow shovels and saws; tents; a two-way radio and extra batteries; a signal device such as smoke or rocket-type flares, signal mirrors or portable emergency locator transmitters; an adequate number of trail marker wands; crevasse rescue equipment; expedition-quality sleeping bags; rope; sun goggles; medical kits; sleds; and repair kits for the equipment carried.

A climber checks in at the High Altitude Research Station at the 14,300-foot level of Mount McKinley. Doctors at the station research human adaptation to altitude and medical problems such as altitude sickness. (Chlaus Lotscher)

One of the worst hazards for climbers is altitude sickness, a general term used to describe the body's failure to adapt to the stress of high altitude and lack of oxygen. Symptoms range from headache and loss of appetite to shortness of breath, rapid heart and breathing rate and even progressive deterioration leading to coma and death. There is no way to predict who will or will not develop altitude sickness; physical fitness offers absolutely no protection from it. The best treatment is rapid descent for acclimatization at a lower altitude. Even better is prevention, accomplished by maintaining a safe rate of ascent, not pushing yourself and allowing adequate time to acclimatize at 14,000 feet or so before moving up higher on the mountain. Carrying loads high and returning to sleep at lower elevations is also considered helpful.

Other physiological and physical hazards of high-altitude climbing include frostbite, hypothermia and dehydration. With proper protection, none of these need occur. Mountaineers should also be aware that the altitude and lack of oxygen can have unusual effects, such as physical weakness, diminished mental capacity and a lack of motivation.

Anyone serious about climbing Mount McKinley should obtain more specific information from the Mountaineering Ranger, Denali National Park and Preserve, P.O. Box 588, Talkeetna, AK 99676.

A History of Mining in the Kantishna Hills

By Thomas K. Bundtzen

Editor's note: A frequent contributor to the *ALASKA GEOGRAPHIC*®, Tom is a geologist for the state Division of Geological and Geophysical Surveys in Fairbanks. This article is taken in part from one which originally appeared in *The ALASKA JOURNAL*® in spring 1978.

The Kantishna (or *Khenteethna* in Athabascan) Hills, a northeast-trending range of hills in the northern portion of Denali National Park, are separated from the main crest of the Alaska Range by the Clearwater Fork of the Toklat River. To outdoor enthusiasts this is the site of Camp Denali, a high-quality wilderness camp. The area offers opportunities for

The Stampede antimony mine and mill is nestled in rolling hills of the Kantishna District. By 1941 this mine was the largest antimony producer in Alaska.
(Thomas K. Bundtzen)

hiking, skiing, berry picking, wildlife observation and a spectacular view of Mount McKinley. To miners, however, the Kantishna Hills are noted for coarse placer gold, bonanza-grade lead-silver ores and Alaska's largest antimony producer at Stampede.

Before the mining era began, the Kantishna Hills were known to native Athabascans and explorers as the Chitsia Hills or Chitsia Range, named after a distinct northern promontory, Chitsia Mountain. Chitsia means "heart" in Athabascan and specifically meant "moose heart" to native hunters of the area. Chitsia Mountain plays a role in an Athabascan legend about the formation of Mount McKinley. It has always been a landmark to Natives, explorers and miners.

The first inhabitants of the area did not know that approximately 85 to 105 million years earlier the layered

rocks of the Kantishna Hills, after undergoing several periods of thermal metamorphism and plastic brittle deformation, warped into broad, northeast-trending folds. Along the crest of one particular fold, the Kantishna anticline, the rocks fractured longitudinally and small bodies of magma were intruded. Subsequently, quartz-carbonate-sulfide veins containing minerals of antimony, silver, zinc, copper, lead, tungsten and free gold were deposited in these fractures. Erosion and geologic time mined and milled countless tons of these veins and concentrated placer gold and sulfide minerals in adjacent stream gravels. In areas of higher vein density, more gold was concentrated, particularly when stream gravels were not diluted by recent Pleistocene glaciation.

Interior Alaska was the scene of a continuing gold rush from the 1880s through the turn of the century. Partly

Carmen Jefford Fisher points out a seam from the Healy coal bearing group. Burned out portions of the seam appear brown. Coal can spontaneously combust and seams sometimes burn for years, leaving behind burned clay and ash. Usually, well-preserved leaf fossils can be found in the burned clay.
(Thomas K. Bundtzen)

because of this extensive mining activity, a number of government expeditions, including those of Frederick Schwatka, Henry T. Allen and Joseph Herron of the War Department, and Alfred H. Brooks of the U.S. Geological Survey, explored the Kantishna River basin and central Alaska Range. When the Honorable James Wickersham, judge of Alaska's Third Judicial District,

attempted to climb Mount McKinley in 1903, he inadvertently discovered placer gold in the stream gravels of Chitsia Creek in the northern Kantishna Hills (then Chitsia Hills) and promptly staked four claims, recording them at Rampart upon his return. Ironically, Chitsia Creek would never have a recorded production of gold. Wickersham's enthusiasm for the area and its gold potential did generate interest among prospectors in the Yukon-Tanana region, who were ready to stampede to any new creek where they suspected gold. Thus in 1904 a number of prospectors began searching foothills of the central Alaska Range for gold. Among them were two that would figure in Kantishna's history: Joseph Dalton and Joseph Quigley. The

following is excerpted from "Mineral Resources of the Kantishna Region" (1918) by Stephen R. Capps, a U.S. Geological Survey geologist:

In 1904 Joe Dalton and his partner Reagen prospected in the basin of the Toklat River and after having found gold in encouraging amounts, returned to Fairbanks that fall. The next spring Dalton and another partner, Stiles, returned to the Toklat and prospected Crooked Creek, a tributary heading in the Kantishna Hills.... In the summer of 1905 two other prospectors, Joe Quigley and partner Jack Horn, had been told by trappers that there was gold on Glacier Creek, and they came in to investigate. They found gold in paying quantities, staked the creek, and in June of that year carried the news of their discovery to Fairbanks and so started the stampede to Kantishna. The stampeders began to arrive about July 15, 1905....

Dalton and Stiles had heard nothing of the stampede and met many treasure seekers shortly after they staked their discovery claims on Friday and Eureka creeks. During the fall and winter of 1905 the Kantishna area was the scene of great excitement. Several thousand people traveled up the Kantishna River, a tributary of the Tanana, by boat during the season of open water and by dog sled on the winter ice.

Capps further states: "Practically every creek that heads into the Kantishna Hills was staked from source to mouth and intervening ridges were not ignored." Within weeks, several towns were constructed, the largest of which were Glacier City, on the Bearpaw River; Diamond, at the mouth of Moose Creek; and Roosevelt and Square Deal on the Kantishna River. In every settlement, there were hastily constructed saloons and gambling establishments, usually housed in wall tents, to facilitate the miners' needs. As in so many mining stampedes, "mining the miner" became the most lucrative business. Eureka, located near many of the active paystreaks, became the summer mining camp. According to Fannie Quigley, a long-time resident of the area, there were approximately 2,000 people in Eureka in 1905. During the fall of 1905 river steamers served Roosevelt and Diamond. Passengers and freight were carried at $50 per person and $40 per ton, respectively.

Miners working two paystreaks on Eureka and Glacier creeks were highly successful and undoubtedly made their fortunes, but little rich ground was to be found on Friday, Glenn, Rainy, Moose, Caribou, Spruce, Stampede, Crooked and Little Moose creeks. This soon became evident to the many prospectors who had rushed into the district, and by spring 1906, a mass exodus occurred as numerous disappointed treasure seekers left the area. Charles Sheldon noted that both Roosevelt and Diamond were emptying fast in May and June 1906. About 35 to 50

Vertically oriented quartz-sulfide-gold veins intrude rocks of the Yukon Crystalline Terrane in the Kantishna District. Veins like this are the source of gold in the Kantishna and Bonnifield districts of the central Alaska Range. (Thomas K. Bundtzen)

men remained to work the paystreaks in the Kantishna district. (This relatively low level of placer mining has continued, with sporadic interruption, to the present day.) The permanent inhabitants resided in Eureka, temporarily named Shamrock City in 1918, during the summer and moved north to Glacier, Roosevelt and Diamond in the winter, where timber and big game were abundant. A few of the miners, among them Joe and Fannie Quigley, stayed in Eureka year-round, particularly after the silver mining period of the 1920s. Beginning in 1909 a permanent recording office was established at Eureka.

As in many mining camps of that era, the creeks, rivers, lakes and prominent topographic features were named quickly. Grant Pearson, a former superintendent of Mount McKinley National Park and long-time resident of Alaska,

This folded schist is visible along Crooked Creek in the Kantishna Hills. Laboratory work studying garnets and other minerals suggest this area shows the highest grade of regional metamorphism in Denali National Park. (Thomas K. Bundtzen)

relates in *My Life of High Adventure* (1962) that Wonder Lake was not named by an awe-struck explorer gazing at McKinley's reflection. Apparently, when two prospectors emerged from the heavy spruce forest (known for years as the Big Timber), and came upon the four-mile-long expanse of water, one miner said, "I wonder how we missed this before." With frontier humor prevailing, the lake became "I Wonder Lake." The "I" was later dropped.

Of the Alaskan pioneers who lived in the Kantishna area, perhaps the best known are Joe and Fannie Quigley. Fannie, known affectionately as "Fannie the Hike," came to the North Country to escape a less-exciting life in rural Nebraska. Arriving with thousands of

Moose hunters (left to right) Fannie Quigley, Joe Quigley, Ruth Wilson and Joe Dalton pose at the head of Bear Creek in this undated photo. Dalton and the Quigleys were longtime residents of the Kantishna area, arriving in the early 1900s in search of gold. Joe and Fannie made many mineral discoveries in the district, the richest of which was the Red Top Mine. (Stephen Foster Collection, University of Alaska Archives; reprinted from The ALASKA JOURNAL®)

the Territory's few gourmet cooks.

Joe Quigley first entered Alaska through Chilkoot Pass in 1891, years before the larger interior gold strikes, but finally ended up living off the land in the Kantishna district. He is remembered as a good prospector and self-taught scientist who enjoyed reading and gardening.

A subsistence hunting ethic evolved among the residents of the Kantishna area and some market hunting was done to keep the mining camps supplied. The Quigleys spent considerable time hunting. In 1908 they hunted Dall sheep near Polychrome Mountain, in present-day Denali National Park, with Charles Sheldon, who recalls in his book, *The Wilderness of Denali* (1960), "I went hunting with Mrs. Quigley and after an arduous climb, which she made as easy as any man, we came close to a band of 34 sheep. . . . The Quigleys came back with two ewes and a yearling ram, quite delighted with this supply of sheep meat to take to their mining cabin."

During summers, several of the mining camps maintained gardens on south-facing slopes above timber line. Although soil and water had to be

other fortune hunters in the days of '98, she started out as a dance-hall girl in Dawson City and later cooked for miners during a number of stampedes. Fannie could sense a new strike in the making. She would arrive beforehand by boat or dog sled with the tools of her trade: a Yukon stove, tent, food staples, firearms for hunting meat and a sign that read:

"Meals for Sale." When another strike came along, she would pull her tent and start in the appropriate direction. Her last stampede was Kantishna, where she met and married Joe Quigley and settled down. Her fame continued to spread, and when she died in 1944, she was known as dog musher, prospector, trapper, hunter, gardener and one of introduced from floodplains and creeks, these gardens were often quite successful. Fannie Quigley fed a number of the miners with home-grown vegetables from her garden overlooking Friday Creek. She would often amaze winter visitors by serving fresh produce during cold winter days, made possible by storage in a natural refrigerator, a permafrost tunnel near her cabin.

The immediate discovery of pebble- to boulder-sized galena (ore of lead) and stibnite (ore of antimony) in the sluice boxes of the early miners prompted a successful search for hard-rock mineral deposits. Likewise, the high price of antimony during the Russo-Japanese War (1904-1905) led Joe Quigley to ship 12 tons of stibnite ore from the Last Chance Mine on Caribou Creek; thus began the development of lode mining in the Kantishna mining district.

Joe Quigley began prospecting the region shortly after the initial stampede and soon found a number of lead, zinc, silver, gold and copper-bearing veins on what was known during the early years as Mineral Ridge, now known as Quigley Ridge. From 1907 to 1909, Tom Lloyd and partners prospected in the Glenn Creek area and made a number of hard-rock discoveries. In 1910, Lloyd, William Taylor, Charles McGonagall and Pete Anderson formed the Sourdough Expedition, the first to successfully climb the North Peak of Mount McKinley. After coming off the mountain, Tom Lloyd and partners developed an antimony deposit on Slate Creek and eventually produced 125 tons of high-grade ore in 1916.

Long-time Kantishna residents Joe and Fannie Quigley built this cabin on Moose Creek near their gold claims. (Steve McCutcheon)

By 1919, mineral veins containing sulfides of antimony, lead, silver, arsenic, zinc, copper and free gold were located along a belt that extended 35 miles from Slate Creek through Stampede Creek. Much of the best ground was staked by Joe Quigley. Although Quigley was an outstanding prospector, he evidently was not an experienced hard-rock miner, since production of high-grade lead-silver ores did not begin until a number of the Quigley properties were leased to Tom P. Aitken and Hank Sterling. From 1919 to 1924, 1,435 tons of ore were taken from eight small deposits on Quigley Ridge and Alpha Ridge. These ores contained 253,000 ounces of silver, at least 450 ounces of gold, and perhaps 750 tons of by-product lead and zinc. Even at the lower metal prices of these earlier years, the ores were worth about $300,000 and their development generated interest in the mining and geologic communities.

During 1920 the Quigleys discovered lead-copper-zinc deposits at Copper Mountain, now Mount Eielson, in the national park. (This mining development can be seen with binoculars from Eielson Visitor Center.) Several hundred men rushed in to stake the several-mile-long lode, but activity eventually waned.

In summer 1924, Carl Ben Eielson flew a World War I Jenny to Copper Mountain. With no airstrip available, Eielson made a bumpy landing on the floodplain of the Thorofare River. This was one of the first gravel-bar landings in Alaska and Ben gained instant fame. When he was killed in a 1929 crash, the miners renamed Copper Mountain, Mount Eielson, in his honor.

The broad lowland that separates the front ranges from the central
Alaska Range highland (the first 15 miles of the park road) is the trace
of the Hines Creek Strand of the Denali Fault, one of North America's
largest transcurrent fault features. The system is more than 1,500
miles long and juxtaposes rocks of the Yukon Crystalline Terrane on
the north (at right in photo) against younger rocks of the McKinley
Terrane to the south. (Thomas K. Bundtzen)

Unfortunately for the silver miners of the 1920s, the Kantishna district had a serious transportation problem and the silver ores were expensive to develop. After being sacked they were transported in late winter from Eureka to Glacier City. From there the ores were hauled by horse-drawn sleds over a 22-mile corduroy wagon road to Roosevelt, where they awaited spring breakup. Then a steamer barged the ores down the Kantishna River to the Tanana, eventually reaching St. Michael at the mouth of the Yukon River. The ore shipment finally made it to Tacoma, Washington, by way of ocean steamer. The cost of transporting ore from mine to smelter was $75 a ton — an uneconomic trip unless the silver assay was at least 100 ounces a ton; silver was worth nearly $1 an ounce in 1920. On completion of the Alaska Railroad in 1923, mining supplies were brought into the district along a winter sled road from Kobe at railhead (near the present Nenana River Bridge crossing on the Parks Highway at Rex), then west across the northern edge of the foothills to Diamond. From there a trail led to Glacier and Eureka.

Some differences of opinion developed between Quigley and Aitken about the terms of the leases on the Quigley Ridge silver properties. These were not resolved, and in 1922 Aitken and Sterling left the district. This, coupled with the apparent exhaustion of easy-to-find, high-grade lead-silver ores, spelled the decline of this early hard-rock mining. Placer mining also decreased, and by 1925 only 13 miners were recovering gold from their sluices in the Kantishna district.

During this early lead-silver mining period, two larger-scale hydraulic placer mines operated, but both proved to be unsuccessful. The Kantishna Hydraulic Company controlled 890 acres of bench gravel on Moose Creek above the mouth of Eureka Creek. An elaborate system of five giants, or monitors, stripped unthawed gravels into a long line of sluice boxes. For this project, a 12,000-foot-long ditch, six feet wide and two feet deep, was built from Wonder Lake to the mine site. In addition, a dam was constructed at the lake to build up a water head for the ditch. Seven men worked eight-hour shifts during summer 1922 and reportedly cleared 50,000 square feet of gravel 10 feet deep. Gold recovery was below expectations and the project was abandoned. In the same year, the Mount McKinley Hydraulic Company used three giants to develop a similar placer gold deposit on upper Caribou Creek. A five-man crew cleared 70,000 square feet of gravel six to eight feet deep, but failed to show a commercial return. As John Davis, a territorial mine inspector, stated: "No data could be obtained as to the amount of gold recovered, except that it was somewhat disappointing."

As mining waned in the southern district, placer gold deposits on Crooked Creek, Joe Dalton's initial discovery, received renewed attention. In 1924, Dewey Burnett and Margaret Hunter began mining a large bench on Crooked Creek several miles below its source. This operation continued sporadically until 1965. Small-scale gold mining also took place on Little Moose Creek and Stampede Creek during the 1920s.

In 1931 Joe Quigley began tunneling into one of his claim blocks, the Banjo claim, at the 3,860-foot elevation on Iron Gulch. A cave-in occurred and he suffered major injuries. Although this accident essentially ended Quigley's career as an underground miner, he recognized

Fannie Quigley and other long-time residents of the Kantishna area were justly proud of their gardens. Fresh vegetables offset a diet of meat, and flowers brightened a long day of toil in rough country. (Alissa Crandall)

that the large and continuous Banjo quartz-sulfide vein consistently yielded $15 to $18 per ton of free gold from panned crushed ore. This vein would become the largest tonnage hard-rock producer in the Kantishna district.

Economic conditions improved in Alaska when President Franklin Roosevelt raised the price of gold to $35 an ounce, and the gold mining industry

57

boomed during the Depression. Kantishna was no exception. A secondary road (the present park road) from the Alaska Railroad to Eureka was completed in the late 1930s, easing the transportation problem that had plagued the district.

In 1935 a group headed by A. H. Nordale, E. Gustafson, C. M. Hawkins and others gathered considerable capital and formed the Red Top Mining Company (named after the Red Top Mine, Quigley's richest find) in hopes of developing a mine in the Kantishna. They acquired 17 patented claims, most of them in the Quigley Ridge area. Exploration was begun on the Banjo vein in 1936. Diamond drilling and tunneling blocked out a large reserve of commercial-grade mineralization, and by the end of 1938, seven miles of road, an airport, a 24-ton-a-day ball mill, assay shop, bunkhouses, blacksmith shop and other structures were assembled. A mill test of an unknown but significant amount of ore, completed in 1938, turned out satisfactory results. Full-scale production began in 1939 and by the time it ended in summer 1942, 6,259 ounces of gold, 7,113 ounces of silver and 40,000 pounds of by-product lead and zinc had been gleaned from 13,655 tons of ore.

Kantishna's placer boom began during the same time that the Banjo vein was being developed. The Carrington Company of Fairbanks leased ground from Denali climber William Taylor on Caribou Creek near the site of the 1922 Mount McKinley Hydraulic Company operation. According to Arthur Erickson

Earl Pilgrim, shown here in 1980 at age 88, acquired the antimony claims at Stampede in 1936. Transportation for ore had always been a problem for Kantishna miners, and in 1941 Pilgrim built an airstrip and shipped out ore by plane to Nenana. Pilgrim passed away in 1987. (Thomas K. Bundtzen)

of the Carrington Company, "[The] equipment consisted of what some people call a dragline and others a dry-land dredge. It had a trommel screen, a sand elevator, a belted stacker for tailings, and regular dredge tables for recovery. It was fed by a $1^3/_4$-yard dragline. The dredge was mounted on crawlers similar to a tractor and was pulled ahead by the tractor or the dragline. Our records show that we put through 75 yards per hour including moving time or other delays during the season." The plant was designed by the Carrington Company, with the help of the Washington Iron Works, who built it.

With 10 men working two 10-hour

shifts day and night, gold production varied between 200 and 300 ounces a week. During the three full seasons of operation, 1939 to 1941, 3 million bedrock feet of gravel, were processed through the washing plant.

Development work on the Stampede antimony deposit commenced in 1916 and again in 1926, but it was not until 1936 that Earl R. Pilgrim acquired the claims at Stampede from old-timers Taylor, Drayton and Trundy. Pilgrim and Morris P. Kirk and Son, Inc., a subsidiary of National Lead Company, began active mining in winter 1936, and by 1941 the Stampede deposit was the largest antimony producer in Alaska. The discovery, made shortly after the turn of the century, consisted of a spectacular vein of nearly pure stibnite 26 feet wide. Although considerable antimony ore had previously been developed in the Fairbanks district, and to a much lesser extent in the Nome and Kantishna districts, it wasn't until after the 1930s that prices allowed for more remote deposits like Stampede to be developed.

Stampede shipped ore on a fairly continual basis until 1970. Roughly two-thirds of the total 3,700 tons of high-grade ores and concentrates, containing 52 percent or more antimony, were shipped

Located on the Kantishna River, Roosevelt was one of the early mining supply camps of the Kantishna District. During fall 1905, river steamers served the community, carrying freight for $40 per ton and passengers for $50 per person. Today, a few weathered buildings are all that remain of the once-thriving community. (Ron Dalby)

The historic Kantishna Roadhouse stands as a reminder of more active days in the Kantishna mining district. (Jerrianne Lowther, staff)

out in the winter along the 56-mile-long Stampede Trail by tractor-pulled sleds. Usually one tractor hauled 40 tons of sacked stibnite (antimony sulfide), but two would often team up to negotiate hazardous areas.

Although consultants told Pilgrim that it would not be economical to build an airport and ship out ore by airplane, he defied their advice and in 1941 constructed a 1,100-foot-long airstrip (later expanded to 4,000 feet) on an elevated floodplain on the Clearwater Fork of the Toklat River. Beginning in 1947 the first 40-ton ore shipment was flown to Nenana in one-ton loads using a Norseman plane. Later, C-46 aircraft hauled out the ores in five-ton shipments.

Earl Pilgrim referred to some of the miners who have worked for him throughout the years as "stakers," men looking for a grubstake. These men were often highly skilled and hard working, rarely missing a round a day. (A round is a mining term for the excavation, drilling and blasting of a certain amount of rock at the face of a vein or orebody. Before modern technology, it usually took an entire shift to complete a round; with today's equipment, several rounds can be completed per shift.) But as the months dragged on, the stakers would get cranky and irritable, longing for comforts or dreaming of some future prospecting venture. When he reached this point, the miner would either quit or get fired and catch the next plane out of Stampede. Months later, however, the same man might show up at Stampede again, and Pilgrim would, of course, rehire him.

The late 1930s and early 1940s certainly could be considered a golden era for the district with its three all-time largest mines operating and the usual small placer deposits being worked. Stampede actually accounted for a considerable percentage of U.S. domestic antimony production during this time.

World War II changed the complexion of Alaska mining dramatically. Ironically, the man who helped stimulate the boom of the 1930s, Franklin Roosevelt, also helped end it: a federal order shut down gold mines throughout America because gold extraction was considered nonessential to the war effort. The Banjo Mine ceased operations, never to resume. The generating equipment of the Caribou Creek dry-land dredging operation was dismantled and removed for the war effort. Strategic metals like antimony were in demand and the Stampede and Slate Creek deposits shipped several hundred tons of ores and concentrates, although manpower shortages created by the war hindered production.

After the war, mining in the Kantishna Hills began a downward spiral. Inflation skyrocketed mining costs but the price of gold remained the same. Newer higher-paying jobs connected with Alaska's post-war military build-up made "good mining men" hard to find. During the 1950s and 1960s, mining in the Kantishna Hills consisted of limited shipments of ore from Stampede, and to a lesser extent Slate Creek, plus a handful of small-scale placer operations.

In 1960 the Alaska Road Commission budgeted $250,000 to construct a transportation corridor into the district from the railroad via Stampede. Work ceased the following year and today the Stampede Road is partially overgrown and unused.

A private company and the U.S. Bureau of Mines conducted exploration for silver and other metals on Quigley Ridge from 1960 to 1962, but failed to locate a large commercial orebody. Drilling programs subsidized by the federal government in search of strategic minerals did locate additional antimony reserves at Stampede and Slate Creek, resulting in further mineral production.

During the 1970s, mining activity increased as a result of the rapid rise in the price of gold beginning in 1972. Modern mechanized placer mining, using bulldozers and front-end loaders, worked gravels that either had been

mined in earlier years or were not accessible in the past. Renewed interest in the Quigley Ridge silver deposits in 1973 led a lessee of the Gold Dollar claim to construct a 35-ton-a-day flotation mill at the Red Top Mine, just above the Friday Creek airstrip. More than 100 tons of ore were mined, milled and shipped to a British Columbia smelter. High antimony prices from 1970 to 1972 prompted ore shipments from the Stampede, Slate Creek and Last Chance Creek deposits.

Total known production of metallics from the Kantishna Hills from 1905 through 1985 has been modest, amounting to 99,646 ounces of gold, 308,716 ounces of silver, about 5 million pounds of antimony and approximately 1.5 million pounds of combined lead and

Fannie and Joe Quigley and other early residents of Kantishna hunted Dall sheep to stock their own larder and sometimes to sell to others. (W.E. Ruth)

zinc. It appears that the Kantishna Hills area could continue to produce metals on a rather small scale, as it has for more than 80 years. Possibly with improved mining techniques and exploration, new and known deposits could be worked economically at larger scales than in the past.

Kantishna's mining heritage should never be lost, for its color shows up not only in its beautiful creeks, hills and wildlife, but also in its miners, and in the lives of the "men [and women] who have moiled for gold."

Riding the Rails to Denali Country

Denali country and the Alaska Railroad go hand in hand. Mount McKinley and Denali National Park top the attraction list for railroad passengers, and in the years before 1957 when the Denali Highway opened, riding the rails was the most common way of reaching the high mountain wilderness of Denali. Not until completion of the George Parks Highway in 1971 was McKinley Park Station easily accessible to the motoring public.

The Alaska Railroad and Denali National Park grew up together. When President Warren Harding drove the golden spike at Nenana signifying com-

Diesel rail cars of the Alaska Railroad make flag-stop runs into Denali country to serve residents of the area who would have a difficult, cross-country journey to reach the George Parks Highway. Here the train picks up passengers and freight at Talkeetna. (Chas. P. Jones)

pletion of the railroad on July 15, 1923, the fledgling park (known until 1980 as Mount McKinley National Park) was just getting going. The park and railroad have matured, the one becoming the most visited attraction in the state, and the other developing into an efficient, modern railroad, the most northerly on the continent.

The rugged terrain of Denali country provided some of the most challenging obstacles for railroad engineers and construction crews, but their success in overcoming these obstacles helped break the isolation of the Interior.

Engineers first tackled Denali terrain in winter 1917 when they set up camp near Dead Horse Hill. The area later became known as Curry in honor of Congressman Charles F. Curry of California who, as chairman of the Committee on Territories, enthusiastically supported Alaska and the railroad.

From here crews pushed farther up the Susitna Valley, snaked through narrow Indian River valley, squeezed through the area known as Canyon, and finally rounded the northern end of Curry Ridge to meet Mount McKinley head on. Beyond, the landscape opened across Broad Pass until it once again constricted the route through narrow Nenana Canyon and out onto the lowlands of the Tanana River valley. Later, Curry became the center for changing train crews, and for tourism with construction of a hotel there. Visitors could ride the train to Curry, stay over at the hotel, take the tram across the Susitna River and climb Curry Ridge for an unforgettable view of Mount McKinley.

Moving men and equipment by boat on the Susitna River system, by horse-drawn sleds and Caterpillar tractors and trailers, construction crews pushed the railbed and tracks farther.

*Railroad crews and residents unload freight at Talkeetna, mile 227
from Seward and the end of steel on March 4, 1919. (Alaska Railroad
Collection, Anchorage Museum)*

Right: Railroad workers plan the next assault on Denali country in this photo of the District Engineer H.F. Dose's Office at Dead Horse (Curry) on March 7, 1919. (Alaska Railroad Collection, Anchorage Museum)

Below: Col. Frederick Mears of the Alaska Engineering Commission, John W. Hallowell, assistant to the Secretary of the Interior, and Dr. Alfred H. Brooks, geologist and explorer, investigate the area for the proposed Alaska Railroad track in the Nenana River valley on August 31, 1919. (Alaska Railroad Collection, Anchorage Museum)

When construction called for a train engine and there was no track on which it could run, teams of horses pulled dinkys, small locomotives, overland.

By 1920, only 83 miles separated the ends of track coming south from Nenana and north from Anchorage. True, Hurricane Gulch and Riley Creek had yet to be spanned, but with each mile of track laid, moving equipment and supplies became easier. An outside company was called in to bridge Hurricane Gulch, allowing the first regular train to pass over the span on August 18, 1921, riding nearly 300 feet above the valley

Horses pull dinky No. 4 on sled runners toward Riley Creek on February 17, 1921. The bridges at Hurricane Gulch, over Riley Creek and across the Tanana River at Nenana were the last gaps in the Alaska Railroad track. The first steel for the Riley Creek span was laid in late fall 1921; on February 5, 1922 the entire span was in place. (Alaska Railroad Collection, Anchorage Museum)

floor. By the end of 1921, passengers could allocate a mere four days on the train to travel from Seward to Fairbanks with overnight stops at Anchorage, Curry and McKinley Park Station.

From the beginning, the railroad maintained friendly relations with the national park. Railroad supplies helped McKinley's first superintendent set up his office and residence. Park and railroad officials coordinated the first special run for tourists when the railroad brought a *Brooklyn Daily Eagle* group

Mrs. Ortell and her son and an unidentified man join Peggie Shallow (far right) and dog Spike at the Broad Pass depot and section house in 1947 or 1948. Peggie's parents worked for the railroad and the family lived at Broad Pass for a number of years.
(Courtesy of Peggie Shallow Reynolds)

in July 1923 to watch the formal dedication of the park.

James Steese, when he was appointed head of the Alaska Engineering Commission which managed the railroad, encouraged tourism in Alaska with his "The New Golden Belt Line Tour." This itinerary called for visitors to travel via Alaska Steamship Company, the Admiral Line, Copper River & Northwestern Railway, Galen and Sheldon vehicles along the Richardson route, as well as the railroad in a tour of southcentral and interior Alaska. Visitors stopped at McKinley Park Station for a trip into the national park.

In later years, as more settlers moved into the upper Susitna Valley and as mining flourished in the Peters and Dutch hills south of the Alaska Range, the railroad became the only reasonable means of moving supplies and equipment for the isolated homesteaders.

Today residents living to the east of the state park and Curry Ridge still rely on flagging down the train to get from their remote homes to Talkeetna or Anchorage. The railroad operates diesel rail cars on runs to Hurricane Gulch specifically to handle these passengers.

Passengers can purchase tickets on board for a particular milepost where the engineer stops the cars. At Gold Creek, Harold Larson and his wife Nancy have made their home in the railroad section house for many years. Gold Creek station is one of the few still staffed year-round, an indication of the importance of the railroad to bush residents living in the foothills away from the river. On one typical trip to Hurricane,

passengers boarded at Talkeetna who were taking supplies to their cabin at Chulitna. Nancy Larson and two of her daughters got on at Gold Creek for a short sightseeing run to Hurricane to take photos. For daughter Shelley, this was a break from correspondence study. Several passengers boarded on the southbound run. At Talkeetna, a dog with no owner in tow was carefully stowed in a kennel box in the baggage car for the ride to Anchorage where its mistress was waiting. Residents use the train ride for transportation and as a chance

Right at home in his office in the baggage car, conductor James Allen sees to the passengers and freight boarding and getting off during the flag stop run to Hurricane Gulch. The Alaska Railroad runs the service so residents living east of Denali State Park can reach Talkeetna or Anchorage. (Penny Rennick, staff)

to catch up on news of their neighbors. As engineer Gary Beitinger stopped the cars to pick up passengers, one of the early boarders excitedly remarked, "Gee, everyone is coming out." Indeed, without the Alaska Railroad, coming out would definitely be an ordeal.

Camp Denali

At Home on McKinley's Doorstep

By Celia M. Hunter

Editor's note: After experience ferrying military planes in World War II, studying and tramping Europe in 1947 and 1948, and working with a fledgling tourist company in Fairbanks and Kotzebue, the author and her partner Ginny Hill Wood looked for a place to establish a wilderness tourist camp. Joined by Ginny's husband, Morton S. "Woody" Wood, a former Mount McKinley Park Ranger, the trio began Camp Denali.

"Why in the world would you start a tourist camp clear out at the end of the road, miles from anywhere?"

We sometimes wondered that ourselves during our first years at Camp Denali. The camp was much more an

Ginny Wood and Celia Hunter lived in this cabin for part of the time they operated Camp Denali. (Pete Martin)

adventure than a business, right from the start. It was a partnership, not just among the three of us who brought the idea into being, but also among all of our friends who became involved, among our staff and even our guests.

By choosing a location at the far western end of the single, one-way gravel road through Mount McKinley National Park, we also had to consider the elements in our scheme, and they were something to be reckoned with.

We were naive. We just wanted to create a place where people could come and enjoy an unsurpassed view of Denali, The High One, in a wilderness setting where the accommodations would be in keeping with the land. We envisioned only housekeeping cabins, leaving us free to roam the park back country with our guests.

We learned about the elements the first summer we were open. Heavy

snowdrifts kept the park road closed until June 13, when Ginny Wood and I finally drove our Jeep station wagon up the steep road carved out of the tundra to our chosen site on the high ridge above Moose Creek a couple of miles north of Wonder Lake.

We had located the spot the previous summer when I had come down from Fairbanks searching for some place outside the park boundary where it would be possible to stake some land for a tourist resort. We wanted a place with a view of the mountain, and had found the ridge and a small tundra pond which reflected Denali. We staked the land under the Homestead Act as a Trade and Manufacturing Site which allowed a maximum of 80 acres per staking.

In fall 1951 we had built the log foundations and floors for two tent cabins before we left for the winter. Now we were back, and shortly after we reached camp, Ginny's husband, Woody, and our friend, Wonder Lake seasonal ranger Les Viereck, followed us. We quickly framed up the first of our tent cabin guest accommodations. No sooner was the canvas wall tent draped over the rafters than Bob Rice flew over in his Navion and landed our first three guests on the gravel airstrip four miles away at Kantishna.

We didn't even have a privy built yet, and here were three young women from Juneau who wanted us to provide meals and lodging. One of them was Shirley Meuwissen Coles, now a Juneau attorney.

The first Camp Denali kitchen was a primus stove on the ground in a 10-foot by 12-foot wall tent, and I was the cook. This hadn't been in our plans, but we learned our first lesson about Camp Denali — it had a life of its own, and we had best go with it.

This should have warned us what life running a wilderness vacation camp was going to be like. For the next 25 years, until we finally sold the camp in December 1976 to present owners Wally and Jerri Cole, we were always running to catch up.

Our first bona fide cook was Liz Berry, a University of California classmate of Woody's, who, with husband Bill Berry, became our first staff in 1954. Bill, a wildlife artist, gathered our wood and water, and in between chores did field sketches of animals.

Liz graduated from a primus to a tempermental kerosene range in a wood-walled tent cabin which was both kitchen and dining room. We didn't have

An unmistakable sound of wildness, the call of the loon is just one of the potential treats for visitors to Camp Denali. This pair of common loons with their chicks patrol a tundra pond in Denali National Park. (W.E. Ruth)

a permanent building in camp until we put up our log lodge in 1954 and 1955 with logs we cut and peeled near Carlo Creek, at the other end of the park, and hauled out with our 1935 Ford truck.

Our second season, 1953, began with a monsoon which swept into the park from Japan on June 24, bringing warm rain up to 11,000 feet. The melting snow overwhelmed the park road's bridges and culverts, closing the road for more than a month. During that time, we continued to operate, giving our arriving guests a real adventure tour by hauling them out to camp in our four-wheel-drive Jeep, in which we had to ford every stream, including the roaring Toklat River.

Airplanes, both our own and others, were vital during those first years. We used a Cessna 170 at first, but soon switched to a customized Piper Super Cruiser, which fitted the short

Kantishna gravel strip much better. Until 1957, we kept the Piper on floats, moored at Wonder Lake.

Many of our friends and guests flew in. Dick Collins, then manager of the CAA (Civil Aeronautics Authority) at Lake Minchumina, 50 miles northwest of Kantishna, was a frequent visitor. Nancy Lee Baker, a fellow ex-WASP, who had helped Ginny and me operate the first Wien Air Kotzebue roadhouse, often flew in from Fairbanks.

We used the Super Cruiser to fly venturesome guests around Mount McKinley, quite a feat since we had a maximum ceiling of 12,000 feet. We also used it to make air drops to mountain climbing parties at McGonagall Pass. When Austin Post, now a noted glaciologist, was surveying one of the Polychrome glaciers during International Geophysical Year in the late 1950s, I airdropped supplies for his crew. I splattered them all over the glare ice . . . a real fiasco.

Bradford Washburn hired us to do some of his aerial photography flights when he was preparing his contour map of Mount McKinley. He and his wife, Barbara, continue to use Camp Denali as an Alaskan base.

Lowell Thomas Jr. and wife, Tay, were based at Camp Denali in 1958 while he was filming a documentary on bush flying. She subsequently wrote *Follow the North Star* (1960), which included a chapter on camp. Reading that book brought at least one Camp Denali staff member to work for us.

The camp staff usually just happened, like so much else connected

Peaks of the Alaska Range tower over Nugget Pond in this autumn photo. (Ginny Wood; reprinted from A Tourist Guide to Mount McKinley *[1980])*

MOUNT DECEPTION
(also known as Mystery Mountain),
11,826 feet

MOUNT BROOKS,
11,940 feet

MOUNT TRIPYRAMID (consists of East (E),
Central and West (W) Pyramid Peaks), 11,600 feet

(W)   (E)

MOUNT SILVERTHRONE,
13,200 feet

with the place. Our first year, we had the assistance of Joan Hessler, who arrived with a group of Harvard mountain climbers in a hearse they had driven from Boston. Throughout the years, our help was often friends of previous staff, or the offspring of friends. Our cooks were mostly amateurs, good cooks who quickly got the knack of preparing in quantity. Everybody, including the cooks, pitched in to help with whatever was going on at camp.

Sometimes people just happened by and stayed to work for a while. We found two Australians hitchhiking on the park road in 1957, and brought them out to use our low-cost Bedrock tent. Thus we met David Williams and Elaine Scott, who spent the entire summer helping convert Upper Camp from tent cabins to permanent chalets.

That same summer, Garry Kenwood, a tall, lean Korean War veteran from Three Rivers, California, drove into the park in his van. He, too, joined our crew, and thus began an Alaskan experience that culminated in his leading a successful climb of Mount McKinley in 1962.

Mount McKinley National Park in those early days had a close-knit community which included National Park Service people; Camp Denali staff; the few Kantishna miners like Johnny Busia, Bill Julian and Frank Bunnell; the hotel crew; and the Alaska Railroad

Bears are sure to generate excitement at Camp Denali. One memorable bruin thrashed the camp kitchen-dining room-store and managed to set the warehouse on fire. (Jim Shives)

station agents. During our first years in the Kantishna, Johnny Busia lived in his cabin across Moose Creek, and we and our guests would pull ourselves over the stream on his handbuilt tram to sit and listen to his tales of the early days, and drink his homebrew.

We all quickly got to know special people who were in the park because getting there took a bit of doing. Until 1957, when the Denali Highway between Paxson and Cantwell was opened, the only way to the park was by the Alaska Railroad. If a visitor wanted his car to drive over the park road, completed in 1938 from the railroad station to Kantishna, he put it on a flatcar in either Anchorage or Fairbanks, then took the passenger train to the park and waited for his car to arrive.

In 1952, special visitors included Herb and Lois Crisler, who were photo-graphing wildlife in the park for a Disney film. This was before they built their tiny cabin on the Killik River in the Brooks Range, collected five wolf pups, and filmed a documentary of them which Lois described in *Arctic Wild* (1956).

Camp Denali underwent many changes throughout the years. What began as a group of tent cabins clustered around Nugget Pond expanded into Upper Camp and Lower Camp following completion of the Denali Highway. This was the first road link to the Alaska highway system, thus enabling people to drive all the way into the park.

Upper Camp consisted of lodge and kitchen/dining room, all in our one log building at first, plus warehouse, laundry and shower cabin, known as Sluice Box, tent cabins for guests and staff and a cache beside Nugget Pond.

After 1957, we had permanent chalets for guests in Upper Camp, for whom we provided transportation, meals and lodging, and the tent cabins were moved to Lower Camp, scattered along our one-way entrance road and used by guests doing their own house-keeping who often arrived in their own cars.

We had a small store, also in Lower Camp, with camping supplies, a garage, and parking for camp vehicles. We restricted guest cars to Lower Camp, so people in Upper Camp wouldn't be disturbed by cars going up and down the hill at all hours.

We planned our cabins to give guests as much privacy as possible. We continued to use outdoor privies, and each cabin in both camps was supplied with running cold water in plastic pipes outside the cabin. Most of our privies had superb views of the mountain, and guests reported that they were marvelous birding sites.

Our early primitive wash house evolved into the Sluice Box, a combination camp laundry and linen storage plus home-built shower stall, with hot water produced by a huge, surplus Army Cannon heater, wood-fired.

We used an ancient but dependable 1931 Maytag wringer washing machine for the first couple of decades, and the wet laundry was hung to dry on outdoor lines strung on poles. A long stretch of rainy weather could bring a crisis in fresh linen.

In fall 1960, a hungry grizzly discovered our lightly protected kitchen/dining room and the camp store with their tempting stocks of food. The bear had a ball trashing these buildings, helping itself to whatever food it could wrest out of the cans.

Worst of all, the bear got into our warehouse despite a spiked ramp over the front door, and somehow set it on fire, possibly by scraping around some strike-anywhere matches. This destroyed all our stored food and some equipment.

Friends rallied to our assistance, people like Clem Rawert, whom we had found hitchhiking in the park and eventually helped start an upholstery business in Fairbanks. We made a convoy into the park with Clem, Garry Kenwood, Nancy Simmerman and her friend Alison Smith, both Oberlin College graduates who were on our 1960-1961 staff, and others.

With so much help, we soon put the camp to rights, and had extra time to cut and haul down enough logs from the woods above camp to build Romany House, a tiny 8-foot by 10-foot log cabin, for Ginny and Woody's daughter, Romany.

We had to balance many functions during our too-short summer seasons. Camp generally opened by June 8, and closed soon after Labor Day. This was as much time as we could count on the road being open through the park, since the road traverses 4,000-foot-high mountain passes.

We were constantly building during the summer to expand our facilities to keep up with the demand.

Jenu Cole and her friend Tanya Ewbank show off their butterfly collection at Camp Denali. (Pete Martin)

Until 1976, the camp provided the only service station facilities beyond the railroad and hotel area near park headquarters.

We also hauled mail for many of the Kantishna miners in those days, and my ham radio was the only communication link to town. Our plane was frequently used in emergencies, such as hauling mountain climbers with frozen feet to the hospital in Fairbanks.

Don Sheldon, the famous Mount McKinley pilot, often said that he

73

"owned" the south side of Mount McKinley, and Camp Denali "owned" the north side. He used the Kantishna airstrip as an alternate on many flights, and often buzzed camp to have us bring him gasoline to get back over the mountains to his home base at Talkeetna.

Once, he delivered an unexpected bundle. He had flown over camp one morning, dropping a note requesting us to meet him at the airstrip. Ginny and I hopped in the Land-Rover with a couple of people and arrived just in time to have Don jerk his thumb toward an object on the ground and ask us to deliver it to the ranger station.

"It" was a dead mountain climber wrapped in black plastic, six feet tall, 200 pounds, frozen stiff. We wrestled the corpse onto the roof of the Land-Rover, and managed to keep it aboard during the rough trip to Wonder Lake Ranger Station.

Our rewards for operating Camp Denali aren't measurable in money. We never made that much by the time we covered all the costs of running a place so far from sources of supplies. Our rewards came, and still come, from the friendships we made with all the people associated with Camp Denali throughout the years. We have a loyal group of Camp Denali alumni scattered all over the globe, many of whom write us each Christmas, and whom we have visited on our travels.

Canoeists at Wonder Lake, not far from Camp Denali, enjoy calm waters, a clear view of a moose feeding on water plants and Mount McKinley in the distance. (Alissa Crandall)

Ginny Wood, Celia Hunter, and Tom and Diana Wade close camp in this 1967 photo. (Pete Martin)

Camp Denali was an idea ahead of its time. The concept we had when we established those first scattered tent cabins on the blueberry-covered ridge above Moose Creek has become a major facet of the Alaska tourist picture.

Nowadays, wilderness lodges, guided adventure trips by raft, kayak, hiking and backpacking, and natural history-oriented tours enable thousands of people to enjoy an active, involving vacation experience.

We may have been crazy to put a tourist facility way out there at the end of the park road in the Kantishna back in 1951 and 1952, but that collection of buildings on the ridge above Moose Creek is world famous, and counts its guest list from every state and continent, and dozens of countries.

I'm proud to have been in on the beginning, and I'm sure we had the most fun during those early years when we never knew what would happen next.

75

Guide to Denali National Park Road

Editor's note: This information is taken in part from *A Tourist Guide To Mount McKinley* (1980) by Bradford Washburn and *The MILEPOST®* (1988). Whenever discrepancies occur in mileage, figures from *The MILEPOST®* are given. Mountain and pass elevations coincide with those in *Dictionary of Alaska Place Names* (1971) by Donald J. Orth, unless otherwise noted.

The Denali National Park Road joins the George Parks Highway 237.3 miles from Anchorage or 120.7 miles from Fairbanks.

The road is paved to Savage

Originally part of the Nenana River, Horseshoe Lake has been cut off from the river's flow just north of the national park entrance. The George Parks Highway is visible on the right in this view looking north toward the Nenana Canyon and Healy. (Alissa Crandall)

River bridge. Private vehicles may not travel beyond the checkpoint at Savage River Campground without permission. Shuttle buses and tour buses provide transportation along the remainder of the 91-mile road. Shuttle buses are free; tour buses charge a fare. The National Park Service assesses a $3 entrance fee to travel beyond Savage River checkpoint.

Mile 0.2: Turnoff for Riley Creek information center and campground. A new information center slightly farther in on the park road is under construction and expected to open in 1989.

Mile 1.2: Horseshoe Lake trailhead.

Mile 1.4: Gas station, showers, grocery store. No gas available on park road beyond this point.

Mile 1.6: Alaska Railroad's Denali Park Station. Morino walk-in campground 0.3 mile from depot. Denali Park airstrip adjacent. The

park hotel is across from the station.

The road climbs westward along the north bank of Hines Creek.

Mile 3.5: Turnoff to park headquarters amid thick stand of spruce. Sled dog demonstrations held here.

Poplars and spruces grow steadily smaller as the road rises toward the broad pass between the Nenana and Savage river drainages. Flashy, pink fireweed flanks the road in July. Mountains with peaks rising to 6,000 feet parallel the road on the north. On clear days, Mount McKinley is visible 71 miles ahead. Mount Deborah (12,540 feet) rises 60 miles to the rear.

Mile 10.2: View of both peaks of McKinley, flanked by Double Mountain (5,899 feet) on left, Sable Mountain (5,923 feet) on the right. Look for Dall sheep on mountain slopes to the north, and for wild roses in nearby vegetation.

Mile 12.8: Savage River Camp-

77

A group of wolves searches the snow for mice. Denali National Park has about 15 wolf packs, ranging from two to 15 members. (Reprinted from A Tourist Guide to Mount McKinley [1980])

ground and checkpoint. Only vehicles with permits allowed beyond this point.

Approaching Savage River, search rock outcrop on right for marmot and pika.

Mile 14.7: Savage River bridge. To the south, toward the head of Savage River, lower peaks of the Alaska Range, topped by Fang Mountain at 6,736 feet, rise a dozen miles away.

Mile 17: The road climbs over a treeless pass between Savage and Sanctuary rivers, with a last view of Mount McKinley before dropping into the wooded Sanctuary Valley.

Mile 22: Sanctuary River Campground. Sanctuary River bridge. Watch for moose, fox, grizzly and wolf. Mew gulls nest along river bars near here.

The road now swings south, with Double Mountain and 5,000- to 6,000-foot peaks at the head of Sanctuary Valley to the left.

Mile 24: At 2,700 feet, the road crosses a low pass into the broad, forested Teklanika River valley. The river begins 20 miles to the south among lower peaks of the Alaska Range, including Double Mountain, the nearest and highest peak.

Mile 25.3: The road skirts the river, occasionally visible through spruces to the right. Watch for grizzlies on the river bar. Climbing slowly but steadily southward, the road follows the surface of an old river terrace deposited toward the end of the Ice Age.

Mile 29: Teklanika Campground. From here, the road winds through spruces and descends steeply to cross the river.

Mile 31.3: Teklanika River bridge. Look left for a memorable view of Double Mountain and higher peaks at the head of Teklanika Valley. Beyond the bridge, the road follows a level, forested terrace on the west side of the valley. Rounded, tundra-covered peaks and craggy summits rise ahead and to the right.

Mile 32.3: Igloo Mountain (4,751 feet) is best seen from this point. Watch closely for Dall sheep on the mountain's slopes.

Mile 34: Road crosses Igloo Creek. Igloo Creek Campground. Moose, bear and Dall sheep are seen frequently here.

The road squeezes between Igloo Mountain and 4,900-foot Cathedral Mountain on the left. Dall sheep are usually seen grazing on high slopes on both sides of the road. Light-colored

Toklat grizzlies forage in thick willows along Igloo Creek.

Mile 36.5: The road leaves the forested valley to climb the flanks of Sable Mountain (5,923 feet) to Sable Pass.

Mile 38.3 to 42.9 is a wildlife reserve closed to all off-road foot travel within one mile of each side of the road. Watch for grizzlies on both sides of the road, caribou to the south and Dall sheep to the north. Peaks lower than 5,000 feet rise across the upland to the left.

Mile 38.5: Sable Pass (3,880 feet). Mount McKinley comes into view once again just beyond the pass. Multi-hued volcanic hills lie ahead when the road drops into the valley of the East Fork, Toklat River.

Mile 43.4: Bridge over East Fork, Toklat River. Polychrome Mountain (5,790 feet), the Alaska Range and several glaciers are visible across the open country to the south.. The East Fork heads at glaciers flowing off Mount Pendleton (7,800 feet) and runs 40 miles before joining the Toklat River. In the area intersected by the road, the braided river follows numerous, shifting channels with its water level varying dramatically. Warm temperatures raise the level substantially in late afternoon and evening; storms increase the flow at any time of the day. Watch for grizzlies, fox, wolf and caribou in the river valley.

The road climbs the flanks of Polychrome Mountain with a spectacular view of multi-hued hills of Polychrome Pass. Rocks in this area originated from volcanic eruptions during the Cretaceous Period about 100 million years ago.

Mile 45.9: Polychrome Pass (3,700

Stalks of hardy yellow alpine arnica cover this slope in Denali National Park. Denali country usually marks the westernmost extent of this species. (John W. Warden)

feet). The broad valley of the Toklat River appears below. Huge alluvial fans spread out from the mountains, a result of the tremendous flow of meltwater which ran from receding glaciers at the end of the Ice Age. Look for wildflowers in the alpine tundra on the slopes to the north. Golden eagles soar on thermals above the valley. Dall sheep forage on the hillsides; and grizzlies, caribou, wolves and pikas can be seen in the area. Look for marmots on a rocky outcrop about a half mile west of the pass.

Mile 47: The upper 5,000 feet of Mount McKinley once again come into view and the polychromatic surroundings end as the road drops into a lowland of meadows, then rises to breast the

upland between the two forks of the Toklat River.

From here the 8,000-foot peaks just south of Eielson Visitor Center come into view. Highest of these peaks, 8,828-foot Scott Peak commemorates Lt. Gordon Scott, who died in an airplane accident on June 11, 1953, while mapping the area.

Leaving the upland, the road descends into the valley of the main branch of the Toklat River, one of the

largest flowing from the north side of the Alaska Range. The Toklat winds from the mountains to join the Tanana River about 50 miles below Nenana. Divide Mountain (5,400 feet), which separates the East Fork from the main course of the Toklat, rises to the left. Mount McKinley is visible again ahead across the river's gravel bars.

Mile 53: Toklat River bridge. Watch for metal plaques on the right honoring Charles Sheldon and Harry Karstens, both instrumental in the founding of the national park. Mount Sheldon (5,670 feet), largest peak visible downstream on the west side of the river, lies six miles north of here.

Mile 53.7: Toklat Ranger Station.

The road now breaks out of timber and climbs toward Highway Pass, running through tundra-covered terrain for the next 30 miles or so until reaching Wonder Lake where the forests return.

Mile 58.3: Highway Pass (3,980 feet), one of the highest points on the 90-mile route. Watch for long-tailed jaegers in this area, and inspect nearby tundra for alpine flora, particularly luxuriant near here.

Mount McKinley now towers continuously on the horizon. Look for the snow cone atop the South Peak (20,320 feet) and the sharp North Peak (19,470 feet) to the right. Denali Pass (18,200 feet) and Harper Glacier descending from it

A braided glacial stream at this point, the Toklat River flows out of the Alaska Range 85 miles to the Kantishna River.
(George Wuerthner)

lie between the two peaks, which are two miles apart and known collectively as the Churchill Peaks. The huge slope to the right of the North Peak is Wickersham Wall, 14,000 feet high and one of the world's largest precipices. Peters Dome (10,600 feet), immediately to the right of the North Peak, is visible ahead across the crest of Stony Pass.

Caribou, sometimes in large herds, graze on tundra-covered slopes to the south of the road for the next few miles.

Mile 61: From the top of Stony Hill (3,940 feet), Mount McKinley lies less than 40 miles ahead. [**Editor's note:** Sources report varying elevations for the actual highest point on the road and the elevation of Stony Hill overlook in relation to Highway Pass. The elevation given here for Stony Hill overlook agrees with the National Park Service staff and with topographic maps they use.] Mount Mather (12,123 feet), Silverthrone (13,220 feet) and Brooks (11,940 feet) flank McKinley to the left. At Stony Hill overlook, search for wildflowers such as mountain avens and anemone.

Caribou trails crisscross the tundra below, as the road zigzags down the steep sides of Stony Hill. The gray granite mountain with three summits, Mount Eielson (5,870 feet), lies directly in front of Mounts Mather and Brooks in the view from the valley floor at the bottom of the west side of Stony Hill.

Mile 64.5: Another climb brings the road to the summit of Thorofare Pass (3,800 feet) where, for the first time, all of Mount McKinley comes into view. To the south rise sharp peaks surrounding Scott Peak, eight miles away, with Sunset

While shorebirds are normally associated with sea shores and lake fronts, several species such as this lesser golden plover, nest in the highlands of Denali or pass through the area on migration. (Nature's Images)

Glacier flowing to the right. Mount Eielson is three miles directly across the valley through which the Thorofare River flows on its run from Sunset Glacier to McKinley River. Mount Silverthrone and Mount Brooks appear immediately to the right of Mount Eielson, then come McKinley's two peaks and Peters Dome. Mount Mather is hidden behind Mount Eielson.

Mile 66: Eielson Visitor Center. Pioneer bush pilot Carl Ben Eielson made his historic aircraft landing on the gravel bars of the valley below in 1924. After Eielson died in a crash in Siberia, the mountain, which had been known as

Copper Mountain, was renamed Mount Eielson.

Check for raptors soaring above bluffs backing the valley to the north, and for mew gulls and arctic ground squirrels in the parking and picnic area.

The dirt- and tundra-covered snout of Muldrow Glacier blankets the lower end of gravel bars in the valley between the center and the mountains. The glacier completely blocks the valley ahead and forces the Thorofare River into a narrow box canyon near the meadows to the south of the road.

As the road winds gently down from Eielson toward the west, brilliantly colored cliffs of volcanic rock skirted with the rich seasonal green or red of vegetation rise steeply to the right.

Steep slopes now drop off to the gravel bars far below, as, like at Polychrome Pass, the road here is hewn out of precipitous rocky mountainsides for a short distance. Far ahead, the level green lowlands typical of the country north of Mount McKinley come into view for the first time. These lowlands average 2,000 feet in elevation.

Mile 67: Mount Mather reappears, and Sunrise Glacier, counterpart to Sunset Glacier on another side of the mountain, is visible to the east on the northwest slope of Scott Peak.

The road now turns sharply to the right through a grassy pass at 3,350 feet, leaving behind the gravel bars and multi-hued cliffs and entering a rolling grassy upland. It then swings sharply left and starts a steady descent. The blue hills far ahead and to the right lie behind Wonder Lake.

with daily showings of a slide show on the establishment of the park as a wildlife sanctuary in 1917. For early and late arrivals, a computer containing detailed visitor information will be accessible 24 hours a day.

Gift shops, a grocery store, post office, gas station and showers can be found near the Denali Park Hotel.

Activities

Denali State Park offers about 50 miles of established hiking trails leading visitors into the back country. Wildlife viewing and fishing in the clear streams and lakes of the park are also popular.

State Park officials are considering rerouting the southern portion of Troublesome Creek Trail to avoid bear encounters during the salmon spawning season. The existing trail goes through dense alder and willow and follows the creek for several miles. Noise from the nearby creek makes it difficult for people on the trail to warn bears of their approach and increases the chances of surprise and potentially dangerous encounters.

Kayakers and rafters enjoy the white waters of the Chulitna River in summer. In winter, cross-country skiers traverse the park's trails and slopes.

In addition to touring the park by road or plane, Denali National Park and Preserve offers unmatched back-

Hikers spread out along a narrow tundra trail from Eielson Visitor Center to nearby foothills of the Alaska Range. (John W. Warden)

88

country and mountain climbing experiences. Permits for overnight backcountry camping are required and must be returned when the trip is complete. All Mount McKinley and Mount Foraker climbers must register with the park superintendent and those climbing other peaks are encouraged to register.

The National Park Service offers naturalist walks, hikes, evening programs and dog sled demonstrations throughout the summer. Activity schedules are posted at the hotel, campgrounds and park offices. The park concessionaire and others near the park offer guided raft trips and other park adventures.

No license is required to fish in the wilderness area of Denali National Park and Preserve but most rivers in the park are so silt-laden that they don't support fish. Arctic grayling are found in a few clear mountain streams and lake trout are found in Wonder Lake. A state fishing license is required in the park additions and in the preserve. Check with park headquarters for limits and restrictions.

Hunting with a state license is allowed in the preserve portion of the park only and firearms should be inoperative when backpacking in the wilderness areas.

Services for visitors are limited during the winter, but during late winter and early spring when daylight hours are increasing, visitors enjoy skiing and dog mushing in the park.

Cautions

Bears are common in both parks. Cautions and reports of bear activity are posted on bulletin boards and should be taken seriously. National Park Service staff publishes a newspaper, *Denali Alpenglow*, which provides good instructions for traveling safely in bear country as well as other safety tips.

Moose may not look threatening but any animal protecting its young can be dangerous. Some areas may be closed temporarily because of bear or other wildlife activity. Check information boards at Denali State Park and at the Riley Creek Information Center at Denali National Park.

Weather is unpredictable, especially in May and early June and in the fall. Bring clothing for temperatures from 35° to 75° F. Rain gear plus warm clothing, including a hat and gloves are

All visitors must respect Denali country wildlife, particularly female animals with their young. This photographer is much too close to the grizzly sow and her cubs.
(Steve McCutcheon)

essential whether you are going out for a short day hike or backpacking overnight.

Many streams in both parks are influenced by glacial and snow melt. Crossing these streams is treacherous and requires planning and caution. Wearing shoes, using a walking stick, roping together with other group members and loosening backpack straps are important steps in safe stream crossing. The currents are strong and crossing these streams alone can be deadly. Check with park rangers for further information.

Campfires are permitted only in fireplaces in established campgrounds. A stove is recommended for all backcountry travelers.

One would hope that a reminder about trash is unnecessary, but one plastic wrapper blowing across the tundra will not only ruin the wilderness experience for someone else, but can harm the wildlife who call the park home. Pack out all trash when traveling in the back country.

Bibliography

THE ALASKA ALMANAC®, Anchorage: Alaska Northwest Publishing Company, 1986.

The ALASKA WILDERNESS MILEPOST® Anchorage: Alaska Northwest Publishing Company, 1987.

Berg, Henry C. and Cobb, Edward H. *Metalliferous Lode Deposits of Alaska.* U.S. Geological Survey Bulletin 1246. Washington, D.C.: U. S. Government Printing Office, 1967.

Berry, William. *Deneki, An Alaskan Moose.* New York: The Macmillan Company, 1967.

Bishop, Richard. *Subsistence Resource Use in the Proposed North Addition to Mount McKinley National Park.* Fairbanks: Cooperative Park Studies Unit, University of Alaska, 1978.

Boertje, Rodney. "Nutritional Ecology of the Denali Caribou Herd." Master's thesis, University of Alaska, Fairbanks, 1981.

Bowers, Peter. *The Carlo Creek Site: Geology and Archaeology of an Early Holocene Site in the Central Alaska Range.* Fairbanks: Cooperative Park Studies Unit, University of Alaska, 1980.

Brooks, Alfred H. and Raeburn, D.L. "Plans for Climbing Mount McKinley." *National Geographic,* January 1903, pp. 30-35.

Brovald, Ken C. *Alaska's Wilderness Rails.* Missoula, Montana: Pictorial Histories Publishing Company, 1982.

Burford, Virgil. *North to Danger.* Caldwell, Idaho: Caxton Printers, 1969.

Campbell, Nola H. *Tulkeetna Cronies.* Anchorage: Nola H. Campbell, 1974.

Clifford, Howard. *Rails North.* Seattle: Superior Publishing Company, 1981.

Cordova Daily Times. "All-Alaska Review." Cordova, Alaska: 1928, 1929 and 1931.

Dickey, William. "Discoveries in Alaska." New York *Sun,* January 24, 1897, p.[TS]6.

—. "The Sushitna River, Alaska." *National Geographic,* November 1897, pp. 322-327.

Dixon, Joseph. *Birds and Mammals of Mount McKinley National Park.* Fauna of the National Parks of the United States, Fauna Series No. 3. Washington, D.C.: U.S. Government Printing Office, 1938.

Evans, Gail E.H. "From Myth to Reality: Travel Experiences and Landscape Perceptions in the Shadow of Mount McKinley, Alaska, 1876-1938." Master's thesis, University of California, Santa Barbara, 1987.

Franck, Harry. *The Lure of Alaska.* Philadelphia: J.B. Lippincott Co., 1939.

Gilbert, Wyatt. *A Geologic Guide to Mount McKinley National Park.* Anchorage: Alaska Natural History Association, 1979.

Gravel, Sen. Mike. *A Feasibility and Development Study for a Mount McKinley Recreation City.* Presented to the Joint Federal-State Land Use Planning Commission of Alaska, 1973.

Harris, Ann G. *Geology of National Parks.* Dubuque, Iowa: Kendall/Hall Publishing Company, 1977.

Heacox, Kim. *The Denali Road Guide.* Anchorage: Alaska Natural History Association, 1986.

Heller, Christine. *Wild Flowers of Alaska.* Portland, Oregon: Graphic Arts Center, 1966.

Johannsen, Neil. *Denali State Park: A Master Plan.* Alaska Department of Natural Resources, Division of Parks, 1975.

McIntyre, Rick. *Denali National Park, An Island in Time.* Santa Barbara: Sequoia Communications, 1986.

The MILEPOST®, Anchorage: Alaska Northwest Publishing Company, 1988.

Montague, Richard. *Exploring Mount McKinley National Park,* Anchorage: Alaska Travel Publications, 1973.

Morgan, H. Morris. *An Archaeological Survey of Mount McKinley National Park.* National Park Service contract, 1965.

Murie, Adolph. *A Naturalist in Alaska.* Old Greenwich, Connecticut: The Devin-Adair Company, 1978.

—. *The Grizzlies of Mount McKinley.* Scientific Monograph Series No. 14. Washington, D.C.: National Park Service, 1981.

—. *The Wolves of Mount McKinley.* Reprint. Fauna of the National Parks of the United States, Fauna Series No. 5. Washington, D.C.: U.S. Government Printing Office, 1981.

Murie, Margaret. *The Alaskan Bird Sketches of Olaus Murie.* Anchorage: Alaska Northwest Publishing Company, 1979.

Murie, Olaus. *Alaska-Yukon Caribou.* Washington, D.C.: Bureau Biological Survey, 1935.

Pearson, Grant. *A History of Mount McKinley National Park, Alaska.* Washington, D.C.: National Park Service, 1953.

—. *The Taming of Denali.* Los Altos, California: Grant Pearson, 1957.

Pearson, Grant and Newhall, Phillip. *My Life of High Adventure.* Englewood Cliffs, New Jersey: Prentice Hall, 1962.

Potter, Louise. *Wild Flowers Along Mount McKinley Park Road.* Hanover, New Hampshire: Roger Burt, 1972.

Prince, Bernardine LeMay. *The Alaska Railroad, In Pictures, 1914 Through 1964,* Anchorage: Ken Wray's Print Shop, 1964.

Rhode, Elaine. "Birds of Denali." *Alaska* magazine, August 1984.

Sheldon, Charles. *The Wilderness of Denali,* New York: Charles Scribner's Sons, 1960.

Simmerman, Nancy. *Alaska's Parklands, The Complete Guide,* Seattle: The Mountaineers, 1983.

Singer, Francis. *1984 Aerial Moose Survey, Denali National Park and Preserve,* Survey and Inventory Report AR-4-1. Anchorage: Alaska Regional Office, National Park Service, 1984.

Stern, Richard. *Cultural Resource Investigations in the Vicinity of Carlo Creek, Nenana River Valley, Alaska.* Anchorage: Alaska Department of Natural Resources, 1983.

Treganza, Adan. *An Archaeological Survey of Mount McKinley National Park,* National Park Service contract, 1964.

Troyer, Will. *Movements of the Denali Caribou Herd,* Anchorage: Alaska Regional Office, National Park Service, 1981.

Washburn, Bradford. *A Tourist Guide to Mount McKinley.* Anchorage: Alaska Northwest Publishing Company, 1971.

Whitten, Kenneth. "Habitat Relationships and Population Dynamics of Dall Sheep *(Ovis dalli dalli)* in Mount McKinley National Park, Alaska." Master's thesis, University of Alaska, Fairbanks, 1975.

Wickersham, James. *Old Yukon: Tales, Trails, Trials.* Washington, D.C.: Washington Law Book Company, 1938.

Wilson, William H. *Railroad in the Clouds: The Alaska Railroad in the Age of Steam, 1914-9145.* Boulder, Colorado: Pruett Publishing Company, 1977.

Index

Alaska Geographic® Back Issues

The North Slope, Vol. 1, No. 1. Charter issue. *Out of print.*

One Man's Wilderness, Vol. 1, No. 2. *Out of print.* (Book edition available, $19.95.)

Admiralty . . . Island in Contention, Vol. 1, No. 3. In-depth review of Southeast's Admiralty Island. 78 pages, $5.

Fisheries of the North Pacific: History, Species, Gear & Processes, Vol. 1, No. 4. *Out of print.* (Book edition available, $24.95.)

The Alaska-Yukon Wild Flowers Guide, Vol. 2, No. 1. *Out of print.* (Book edition available, $12.95.)

Richard Harrington's Yukon, Vol. 2, No. 2. *Out of print.*

Prince William Sound, Vol. 2, No. 3. *Out of print.*

Yakutat: The Turbulent Crescent, Vol. 2, No. 4. *Out of print.*

Glacier Bay: Old Ice, New Land, Vol. 3, No. 1. *Out of print.*

The Land: Eye of the Storm, Vol. 3, No. 2. *Out of print.*

Richard Harrington's Antarctic, Vol. 3, No. 3. Reviews Antarctica and islands of southern polar regions, territories of mystery and controversy. Fold-out map. 104 pages, $8.95.

The Silver Years of the Alaska Canned Salmon Industry: An Album of Historical Photos, Vol. 3, No. 4. *Out of print.*

Alaska's Volcanoes: Northern Link in the Ring of Fire, Vol. 4, No. 1. *Out of print.*

The Brooks Range: Environmental Watershed, Vol. 4, No. 2. *Out of print.*

Kodiak: Island of Change, Vol. 4, No. 3. *Out of print.*

Wilderness Proposals: Which Way for Alaska's Lands?, Vol. 4, No. 4. *Out of print.*

Cook Inlet Country, Vol. 5, No. 1. *Out of print.*

Southeast: Alaska's Panhandle, Vol. 5, No. 2. Explores southeastern Alaska's maze of fjords and islands, forests and mountains, from Dixon Entrance to Icy Bay, including all of the Inside Passage. The book profiles every town, and reviews the region's history, economy, people, attractions and future. Fold-out map. 192 pages, $12.95.

Bristol Bay Basin, Vol. 5, No. 3. *Out of print.*

Alaska Whales and Whaling, Vol. 5, No. 4. The wonders of whales in Alaska — their life cycles, travels and travails — are examined, with an authoritative history of commercial and subsistence whaling in the North. Includes a fold-out poster of 14 major whale species in Alaska in perspective, color photos and illustrations, with historical photos and line drawings. 144 pages, $19.95.

Yukon-Kuskokwim Delta, Vol. 6, No. 1. *Out of print.*

The Aurora Borealis, Vol. 6, No. 2. Explores the northern lights in history and today; their cause, how they work, and their importance in contemporary science. 96 pages, $7.95.

Alaska's Native People, Vol. 6, No. 3. Examines the worlds of the Inupiat and Yupik Eskimo, Athabascan, Aleut, Tlingit, Haida and Tsimshian. Fold-out map of Native villages and language areas. 304 pages, $24.95.

The Stikine River, Vol. 6, No. 4. River route to three Canadian gold strikes, the Stikine is the largest and most navigable of several rivers that flow from northwestern Canada through southeastern Alaska to the Pacific Ocean. Fold-out map. 96 pages, $9.95.

Alaska's Great Interior, Vol. 7, No. 1. Examines the people, communites, economy, and wilderness of Alaska's rich Interior, the immense valley between the Alaska Range and Brooks Range. Fold-out map. 128 pages, $9.95.

A Photographic Geography of Alaska, Vol. 7, No. 2. A visual tour through the six regions of Alaska: Southeast, Southcentral/Gulf Coast, Alaska Peninsula and Aleutians, Bering Sea Coast, Arctic and Interior. 192 pages, $15.95.

The Aleutians, Vol. 7, No. 3. Home of the Aleut, a tremendous wildlife spectacle, a major World War II battleground, and an important arm of Alaska's commercial fishing industry. Fold-out map. 224 pages, $14.95.

Klondike Lost: A Decade of Photographs by Kinsey & Kinsey, Vol. 7, No. 4. *Out of print.* (Book edition available, $12.95.)

Wrangell-Saint Elias, Vol. 8, No. 1. Alaska's only designated World Heritage Area, this mountain wilderness takes in the nation's largest national park in its sweep from the Copper River across the Wrangell Mountains to the southern tip of the Saint Elias Range near Yakutat. Fold-out map. 144 pages, $19.95.

Alaska Mammals, Vol. 8, No. 2. Reviews in anecdotes and facts the entire spectrum of Alaska's wildlife. 184 pages, $12.95.

The Kotzebue Basin, Vol. 8, No. 3. Examines northwestern Alaska's thriving trading area of Kotzebue Sound and the Kobuk and Noatak river basins. 184 pages, $12.95.

Alaska National Interest Lands, Vol. 8, No. 4. Reviews each of Alaska's national interest land (d-2 lands) selections, outlining location, size, access and briefly describes special attractions. 242 pages, $14.95.

Alaska's Glaciers, Vol. 9, No. 1. Examines in-depth the massive rivers of ice, their composition, exploration, present-day distribution and scientific significance. Illustrated with many contemporary color and historical black-and-white photos, the text includes separate discussions of more than a dozen glacial regions. 144 pages, $19.95

Sitka and Its Ocean/Island World, Vol. 9, No. 2. From the elegant capital of Russian America to a beautiful but modern port, Sitka, on Baranof Island, has become a commercial and cultural center for Southeastern Alaska. 128 pages, $19.95.

Islands of the Seals: The Pribilofs, Vol. 9, No. 3. Great herds of northern fur seals and immense flocks of seabirds share their island homeland with Aleuts brought to this remote Bering Sea outpost by Russians. 128 pages, $9.95.

Alaska's Oil/Gas & Minerals Industry, Vol. 9, No. 4. Experts detail the geological processes and resulting mineral and fossil fuel resources that contribute substantially to Alaska's economy. 216 pages, $12.95.

Adventure Roads North: The Story of the Alaska Highway and Other Roads in *The MILEPOST®*, Vol. 10, No. 1. Reviews the history of Alaska's roads and takes a mile-by-mile look at the country they cross. 224 pages, $14.95.

ANCHORAGE and the Cook Inlet Basin, Vol. 10, No. 2. Reviews in depth the commercial and urban center of the Last Frontier. Three fold-out maps. 168 pages, $14.95.

Alaska's Salmon Fisheries, Vol. 10, No. 3. A comprehensive look at Alaska's most valuable commercial fishery. 128 pages, $12.95.

Up the Koyukuk, Vol. 10, No. 4. Highlights the wildlife and traditional native lifestyle of this remote region of northcentral Alaska. 152 pages, $14.95.

Nome: City of the Golden Beaches, Vol. 11, No. 1. Reviews the colorful history of one of Alaska's most famous gold rush towns. 184 pages, $14.95.

Alaska's Farms and Gardens, Vol. 11, No. 2. An overview of the past, present and future of agriculture in Alaska, with details on growing your own vegetables in the North. 144 pages, $12.95.

Chilkat River Valley, Vol. 11, No. 3. Explores the mountain-rimmed valley at the head of the Inside Passage, its natural resources, and the residents who have settled there. 112 pages, $12.95.

Alaska Steam, Vol. 11, No. 4. Pictorial history of the pioneering Alaska Steamship Company. 160 pages, $12.95.

Northwest Territories, Vol. 12, No. 1. In-depth look at the magnificent wilderness of Canada's high Arctic. Fold-out map. 136 pages, $12.95.

Alaska's Forest Resources, Vol. 12, No. 2. Examines the botanical, recreational and economic value of Alaska's forests. 200 pages, $14.95.

Alaska Native Arts and Crafts, Vol. 12, No. 3. In-depth review of the art and artifacts of Alaska's Natives. 215 pages, $17.95.

Our Arctic Year, Vol. 12, No. 4. Compelling story of a year in the wilds of the Brooks Range. 150 pages, $12.95.

Where Mountains Meet the Sea: Alaska's Gulf Coast, Vol. 13, No. 1. Alaskan's first-hand descriptions of the 850-mile arc that crowns the Pacific Ocean from Kodiak to Cape Spencer at the entrance to southeastern Alaska's Inside Passage. 191 pages, $14.95.

Backcountry Alaska, Vol. 13, No. 2. A full-color look at the remote communities of Alaska. Companion volume to *The ALASKA WILDERNESS MILEPOST®*. 224 pages, $14.95.

British Columbia's Coast/The Canadian Inside Passage, Vol. 13, No. 3. Reviews the B.C. coast west of the Coast Mountain divide from mighty Vancouver and elegant Victoria in the south to the forested wilderness to the north, including the Queen Charlotte Islands. Fold-out map. 200 pages, $14.95.

Lake Clark/Lake Iliamna Country, Vol. 13, No. 4. Chronicles the human and natural history of the region that many claim has a sampling of all the best that Alaska has to offer in natural beauty. 152 pages, $14.95.

Dogs of the North, Vol. 14, No. 1. The first men to cross the Bering Land Bridge probably brought dogs to Alaska. This issue examines the development of northern breeds from the powerful husky and malemute to the fearless little Tahltan bear dog, the evolution of the dogsled, uses of dogs, and the history of sled-dog racing from the All-Alaska Sweepstakes of 1908 to the nationally televised Iditarod of today. 120 pages, $16.95.

South/Southeast Alaska, Vol. 14, No. 2. Reviews the natural and human resources of the southernmost tip of Alaska's Panhandle, from Sumner Strait to the Canadian border. Fold-out map. 120 pages, $14.95.

Alaska's Seward Peninsula, Vol. 14, No. 3. The Seward Peninsula is today's remnant of the Bering Land Bridge, gateway to an ancient America. This issue chronicles the blending of traditional Eskimo culture with the white man's persistent search for gold. Fold-out map. 112 pages, $14.95.

The Upper Yukon Basin, Vol. 14, No. 4. Yukoner Monty Alford describes this remote region, headwaters for one of the continent's mightiest rivers and gateway for some of Alaska's earliest pioneers. 117 pages, $14.95.

Glacier Bay: Icy Wilderness, Vol. 15, No. 1. Covers the 5,000-square-mile wilderness now known as Glacier Bay National Park and Preserve, including the natural and human history of the Glacier Bay area, its wildlife, how to get there, what to expect, and what changes now seem predictable. 103 pages, $14.95.

Dawson City, Vol. 15, No. 2. For two years just before the turn of the century, writes author Mike Doogan, news from Dawson City blazed like a nova around the world and a million people wanted to go there. Like a nova, the gold-rush burned out quickly, but its light still illuminates the city it built. In this issue Doogan examines the geology and the history of the Klondike, and why a million tourists want to go to Dawson while other gold-rush towns of the North are only collapsed cabins and faded memories. 94 pages, historic and contemporary photos, index, $14.95.

NEXT ISSUE:
The Kuskokwim River, Vol. 15, No. 4. A review of one of Alaska's most important rivers, this issue will focus on the entire Kuskokwim drainage, from the headwaters to the mouth on Kuskokwim Bay. Author Mary Lenz discusses natural and human history along the river, including mining, fishing, riverboats and village life. To members in November 1988. Price to be announced.

ALL PRICES SUBJECT TO CHANGE.

Your $30 membership in The Alaska Geographic Society includes four subsequent issues of *ALASKA GEOGRAPHIC®*, the Society's official quarterly. Please add $4 for non-U.S. membership.

Additional membership information is available upon request. Single copies of the *ALASKA GEOGRAPHIC®* back issues are also available. When ordering, please make payments in U.S. funds and add $1.50 postage/handling per copy. To order back issues send your check or money order and volumes desired to:

The Alaska Geographic Society

P.O. Box 93370, Anchorage, Alaska 99509